Universal Folk Tarot

By Anita Inverarity

10 9 8 7 6 5 4 3 2 1

Made in China

Published by

U.S. GAMES SYSTEMS, INC.

179 Ludlow Street • Stamford, CT 06902 USA

www.usgamesinc.com

Table of Contents

Introduction to Universal Folk Tarot

Anita's personal interest and relationship with the tarot spans more than 30 years. Briefly in the 90s, she offered consultations and workshops in various esoteric arts, but her enduring passion for the cards has been a more personal journey, which she compares to having a good friend on hand with the best advice and nicest teas. Anita knew that one day she would like to illustrate her own deck. That seed was planted in 2012, when the first drawings for Universal Folk Tarot came about.

Following from the publication of her Universal Folk Oracle, Anita describes this new tarot deck as a labor of love, enlightenment and at times, the most extraordinary catalyst for personal growth.

The deck uses the classic Rider-Waite-Smith framework and incorporates occasional alternative narratives from folklore and mythology where Anita felt compelled to bring these stories and illustrations into her tarot journey. As with the Universal Folk Oracle, the delivery is rooted strongly in projecting healing energy and deep compassionate understanding, while still embracing the inherent duality of the tarot. This tarot deck gives plenty of opportunity to work with your shadow in a responsible way and Anita hopes it will appeal to both intuitive readers and those preferring more structure. An additional feature to explore is the inclusion of a crystal companion for each card. Anita has chosen these intuitively throughout the creation of the deck. Each brings a particular medicine and vibration to consider if you are drawn to explore them more.

Major Arcana

0 The Fool

Keywords: innocence; beginnings; adventure; carefree; trust.
Crystal: Hematite: protection; grounding; courage.

The Fool shows a young man setting off out into the world. He is traveling light with just a small knapsack of essentials, as he has not yet accumulated the baggage associated with adult life. The Fool is innocent and pure of heart, his head is filled with big dreams and adventures. He represents our childlike wonder, which we hope to retain on our journey through life. On his cap there is a single feather for pure potential and perhaps also a gift of protection from the angelic realms. The symbol of infinity rests there too, showing his pivotal role in this deck and the Fool's Journey through the Major Arcana. The Fool can appear at the beginning or the end of the Major Arcana cards, showing how the life journey loops around on itself. We start to learn with this card and the more we learn the more we long to be cloaked in the innocence and joy of the Fool card again.

In his belt pouch he carries a tiny, polished hematite stone picked up on his travels. He doesn't fully realize the significance of the stone yet, but it will keep him safe and protected. The Fool may not yet have all the skills to support himself but he is cherished and protected spiritually. If you look closely, you'll notice he wears his heart on his sleeve. The little dog stares in disbelief as he nears the cliff's edge. The sun is shining and he is distracted by the beautiful flowers and billowing clouds without a care in the world. His companion will bark loudly to warn him of any dangers and will stay close by his side for the journey ahead. In the background, there is a hint of night sky, which brings hidden things to fear and the mountains rise up representing challenges to face. The Fool is ready to start his journey of discovery and growth from a place of trust.

Symbolic Healing and Guidance

Ouroboros: infinity; circle of life and death.

Daisy: innocence; purity; birth; new beginnings.

Fairy Ring: veil of forgetfulness; time travel; portals.

Dog: loyalty; trust.

Feather: pure potential; spiritual protection.

Upright Message: There is a particular joy and rejuvenation in your energy at present. It is a wonderful time to start something new with no expectations or real commitment. Exploration, creativity and spontaneous decisions are exciting and favorable. Make time to smell the daisies and enjoy the moment. Take a leap of faith. The timing is right.

Reversed Message: You may need to pay attention to hidden risks and challenges. There is a tendency to be unaware and dreamlike at the moment. Remember to ground your energy and assess new situations or people in particular. Exercise a little more caution in your day-to-day dealings. It is time to slow the brakes and gather your focus while still maintaining the playful energy of the Fool. Pause, play and assess further.

I ☼ The Magician (The Magi)

Keywords: manifestation; alchemy; power; influence; magick.
Crystal: Clear Quartz: transformation; programming; balance.

The magi is mastering his universe and has all the tools at his disposal to manifest his desires. He raises his wand to the heavens, drawing down divine energy to his practice. This is young vital energy awakening to the more experienced energy of the universe as he starts to harness magical powers and alchemy. The Magician is in tune and is an adept, but also fresh and pure of heart. The wand is double tipped with powerful quartz crystals, which helps to transmute and transform energy into matter. There is an understanding of the laws of alchemy and hermetic teachings implying "as above, so below."

On the table, we are introduced to the four symbols of the tarot suits (cups, wands, swords and pentacles.) They also relate to the four directions and elements, the building blocks of life. He wears a cloak of red, symbolizing energy, vitality and action. It is also adorned with suns, moons and stars, showing his assured place in the universe. The magi is becoming aware of himself and his unlimited potential, represented by the infinity loop held over his head. This symbol is echoed again in the spiral shell around his neck. He also wears a pendant of red lava encased in silver to bring balance to his outward masculine traits. The pendant relates to feminine earth energies and the moon (also a balance of the elements fire, earth, air and water). He stands in a fertile garden of his own making with rambling roses and an abundance of lilies. The amanita mushrooms represent elements of chaos and the wild unexpected where science and magick meet paths.

A companion cat gazes into the distance anticipating the next steps for moving forward on the journey. It reminds us that time is more fluid in the magical realms and seeds sown sometimes require patience to mature. There is an indication of rapid growth just ahead.

The crow overhead is a powerful guide through the magical realms. Crow energy has foresight and can communicate hidden knowledge. In many traditions, he is the bird of transformation and change.

The magi is sometimes seen as a shaman or journeyman who can navigate various plains of consciousness. He uses magical knowledge in a very practical and applied manner. He uses his intellect to tap into unseen creative forces and convert it into a resourceful form.

Symbolic Healing and Guidance

Roses: unfolding wisdom; abundance.

Lilies: connection with the divine; hidden realms.

Amanita Mushrooms: chaos in alchemy; factors of the unknown.

Infinity: pure potential; life everlasting.

Cat and Crow: messengers from other realms; time travelers; guardians of esoteric knowledge.

Silver Tools and Adornments: the planet Mercury and quickening.

Upright Message: The conditions are aligned to make your dreams and desires a reality. The building blocks are in place for your endeavors to be successful. The possibility to do great things and gain spiritual wisdom in this next chapter is manifest. Work from the heart and your higher states of consciousness for the greatest good. You are a conduit of unlimited potential.

Reversed Message: This card is a reminder to remain conscious of your powers at this time. Keep your ego in check and other lower human vibrations that you may be tempted to exploit. Many of your realizations will be dizzying and dazzling. Remain grounded and true to your integrity. Clear and cleanse your tools and person daily.

II ✱ The High Priestess

Keywords: intuition; esoteric; secret knowledge; sovereign; divine feminine.
Crystal: Aquamarine: purity; truth; serenity; balance.

The High Priestess sits at the entrance of the temple. The pillars depict the gateway to the Temple of Solomon, which is representative of the "first" temple or the temple we carry within. This priestess encapsulates ultimate purity and divine feminine energies. Her quest is internal, intuitive and mostly hidden from view. Engraved on the pillars are the letters B (Boaz) and J (Jachin) and behind the pillars we see the sun and the full moon depicted. The High Priestess understands the duality of all things and the secrets of both light and dark. The complex workings of the universe are safeguarded by her pureness of being and her lofty position. A manifestation of the divine feminine and a vessel of the great mysteries; her psychic and intuitive powers are highly tuned. While our Magician is busy doing, our High Priestess is concerned with being and receiving.

Her jewels and clothing are of the finest materials. This is not out of a need to show off and be adorned, but to receive the energy of the master craftsmanship contained within each stitch and seam. The crown and jewelry are laden with aquamarine for serenity and truth, pearls for wisdom and ancient ammonites depicting the infinity spiral so often seen in nature. Within her multilayered blue robes she carries sacred texts and amulets stitched inside her hems. Mirroring the Magician, she also chooses the companionship of a crow and cat. This time the white crow in its rarity represents the light, good omens, honesty, cleansing and healing. A small pomegranate pendant is worn around its neck as a reminder of the cycles of life and death. The black cat is representative of the dark, the mysteries and the secrets to be uncovered there.

Symbolic Healing and Guidance

Daisies: purity; virginity.

Mistletoe Vines: sacred protection;
altered states of consciousness.

Cat and Crow: messengers from other realms;
time travelers and guardians of esoteric knowledge.

Crescent Moon: renewal; vow; ritual cleansing.

Sacred Heart: faith and acknowledgment of the divine masculine.

Upright Message: Your intuition and psychic abilities are becoming a strong force that is difficult to ignore. Be still and embrace these innate gifts and learn to trust your inner instincts and outer signs. The High Priestess does not force this nature but will reveal everything you need to know if you remain open and tuned into all possibilities. Be strong of heart and ready to receive revelations.

Reversed Message: Be careful of reveling in your secretive side too much. The priestess energy enjoys speculation and mystery solving as part of her nature. This can be a powerful force for good if transparent and well meaning. Always make sure that the truths from yourself or others are not wrapped up in well-meaning fabrications. Ensure that you enter the temple with only the purest intentions.

III ☼ The Empress

Keywords: beauty; fertility; abundance; maturity; unconditional love; femininity; nurturing.
Crystal: Garnet: love; devotion; beauty and balance.

The Empress sits in her beautiful garden, supported by comfortable cushions and sheltered by rich drapes and tapestries. She is relaxed and aligned with nature, though her nobility is evident in the abundance of jewels and fine clothes she is wearing. Garnets are her chosen stone, earthy, passionate and balancing. They are also linked to the pomegranates springing from the rich soil, a symbol of new life and abundance.

The Empress wears a crown of freshly picked flowers and little green shoots of new growth are prominent in the scene. In her headband she sports twelve garnets, which represent the twelve signs of the zodiac, her celestial subjects and her realm. She has great compassion and understanding for all her people. Ruling over her realm is the planet Venus and unconditional love. Venus can be seen in the night sky and is also depicted in symbolic form on her pillow in the foreground.

The Empress is blooming into full maturity and enjoying the fruits of her success. Two familiars join her under the stars. The owl represents her wisdom and inner knowing. The rabbit represents fertility and feminine energy. This card is all about fertility, creativity, abundant ideas, rich rewards and unlimited potential coming into being. Sometimes, the Empress may be portrayed as pregnant, but she is mostly about nurturing and she is the earthly embodiment of the great Mother Earth deity we recognize in mythology.

Symbolic Healing and Guidance

Pomegranates: new life; abundance; fertility.

Garnets: love; passion; earthly pleasures.

Owl: wisdom; knowledge; growing maturity.

Rabbit: fertility; high energy; creativity.

Venus: love; beauty.

Upright Message: The true road to success is through the beauty of enjoying what this earth has to offer. Indulge in pleasures and self-care. Nature rises and falls regardless of pursuit, so sit back and enjoy its bounty and the more sensual aspects of life. Everything you require is manifest now and is in overflowing abundance. Bless others with your compassion and care as you enter into a period of growth and gratitude for all you have.

Reversed Message: There may be feelings of dissatisfaction or a lack of enjoyment in the things you have around you or your life situation. Those nagging feelings of "never enough" are a call to look at your feelings of scarcity and whether it dominates or causes blocks in your growth. Embrace self-care as the first step; actively enjoy nature, new people and places. Practice feeling blessed and giving gratitude for the small things in life. Try to fill your own spiritual cup first and often.

IV ✱ The Emperor

Keywords: authority; ruler; fatherhood; masculine; discipline; power.
Crystal: Ruby: power; strength; honor; protection.

In contrast to the Empress, we find the Emperor sitting aloof and looking stern. His face is painted in a solemn mask to hide any display of emotion or weakness. He embodies the paternal role of the deck and the requirement to lead and govern. It is a weighty responsibility of his own making, and he chooses a certain level of detachment to fulfill this role. Although they occupy the same garden as divine consorts, the Empress and the Emperor embody different sorts of sovereignty. They are like the yin and yang of the deck: soft and hard, feminine and masculine, passive and active.

The Emperor wears the crown of responsibility. It denotes his status and his spiritual connection, which he wields with a sharp focus and an air of authority. High expectations and moral integrity make him slightly world-weary and he is graying a little on his beard and temples.

The familiars he chooses are both predatory; a white cat who hides sharp teeth in soft fur and the ever-watchful hawk, scoping out his territory and guarding the perimeters.

If the Emperor works from his highest authority, he will carry out his duties with fairness and compassion, leading with strength and intellect. This figure prefers peace and carries a scepter with a blue orb representing a calm, harmonious world. The cloaks and regalia he wears are heavy and formal, yet embellished with crescent moons, an expression of his mystical side. There are jewels and bells hidden in his robes, which he enjoys when able to take some liberty. At any moment, however, he is aware of pending decisions, conflicts and matters to resolve that require him to remain alert and vigilant at all times.

Symbolic Healing and Guidance

Hawk: freedom; protection; divine messages; observation; power; strength.

Cat: solitary; independent; contemplative; aloof.

Star: Sirius the dog star, brightest in the sky; pure intellect and a reminder of the great masculine and divine feminine in the cosmic realms; a source of energy.

Four (number of this card): order; reason; intellect; solid; stability; building blocks.

Three (the red spots on his mask): red for Aries and Mars energy associated with this card; three for skill, creativity and knowledge.

Upright Message: It is time to step into your leadership responsibilities fearlessly but without fanfare. The Emperor card indicates that you are ready, willing and able to rise to any challenge. When you need to take charge, you will do so with fairness and balance. Solutions will be found through reason and intellect. People will feel safe and supported by the decisions you make. You are working with higher energies for the greater good.

Reversed Message: Positions of power may bring situations to exploit or difficult decisions to implement. Take care that you are not moving too far away from your heart center. The Emperor can be cruel and cold when fixated or backed into a corner. He understands more than most the ebb and flow of maneuver and sacrifice. Question your motives and those around you if power plays are making you uneasy. Look out for signs of toxic masculinity, which can manifest in anyone.

V The Hierophant

Keywords: spiritual wisdom; consultation; community; tradition; conformity.
Crystal: Blue Kyanite: guidance; spiritual growth; comfort; healing.

The Hierophant is a respected fountain of knowledge in all aspects of spiritual life. This figure is represented here by the fin wife, who is a wise elder of the sea assuming the body of a beautiful young woman while on land. The tradition of the wise woman or the seer was a strong aspect of community in ancient times before the advent of organized religion. The lighthouse where she resides serves as a beacon to the wider community who seeks her out for counsel and guidance. This embodiment can be seen as an aspect of the High Priestess who is now ready to give up some of her wisdom and secrets. The energy of the card is more authoritative and direct, however, bringing in crone and masculine influences. There is a little bit of smoke and mirrors in her dealings with people, which does not indicate lack of integrity but rather makes the message safer and easier to digest. She displays a raised hand in blessing and carries a cross, both reassuring signs of conformity. Where she is from, the dark and light sit side by side, the veil is thin and the underwater realms are a metaphor for the vastness and depth of our cosmic lessons and understanding.

It is the job of the Hierophant to meet people where they are, to guide and assist where needed. The link to spirit and also messages from the deep are facilitated by her shape-shifting familiar. The cat with the fish tail can quickly swim to and fro, relaying messages from the fin folk under the sea and their council of oracles. The shape-shifting cat is also the keeper of the silver and holds a key to the chest of coins collected. When we meet the Hierophant, we are coming face to face with the manifestation of shared ideas, motivations, exchanges and more organized thought. There is an exploration of what makes people tick and how they congregate to seek further knowledge from each other.

Symbolic Healing and Guidance

Lighthouse: community beacon;
guidance; hope.

Shape-shifting Cat: messenger from
spirit and other realms.

Key: keeper of riches and knowledge.

The Cross and Two Fingered Blessing: signs of conformity; security; reassurance.

Upright Message: The Hierophant as spiritual authority signals a time of study. You have much to gain from the experience of a mentor or tutor. You are seeking new ideas and approaches, but first must have an understanding of the basic ideas that are already held in esteem by the elders and wise sages. Such a meeting will fill your cup and quench your thirst until you can establish your own authenticity and way of being.

Reversed Message: When your mentor or guide appears, there is also an element of great trust. Just because the Hierophant is placed in that position or is indeed very knowledgeable, doesn't mean that their messages may not be contorted by perspective or conditioning. This is a person relaying the divine within their understanding. At some point you will realize that your own wisdom and connection with spirit are just as valuable. The Hierophant reversed signals the need for healthy caution about your chosen authority or expert. It may also point to a conflict or rebellion against conformity and previous trusted sources.

VI • The Lovers (Eden)

Keywords: relationships; values; choices.
Crystal: Rutilated Quartz: truth; self-discovery; awakening; connection.

The Lovers inhabit a beautiful garden symbolic of Eden, or the first paradise on Earth. This is the card of self-discovery. Each of the lovers in turn are witness to each other's true nature and serve as a vow to the divine and a mirror to each other. They are perfection embodied when the divine feminine and the divine masculine come together in harmonious balance. They are involved in a hand-fasting ceremony, committing to one another yet turning away in honor of each other's inner worlds and privacy also. Source energy from the sun breathes downwards and crystalline earth energy rises up in representation of kundalini flow. This union brings excitement and vitality, and the first time to recognize the universe through the eyes of another.

The woman stands under an apple tree where a serpent is climbing the branches. Already she has been distracted by the offer of knowledge and the fruit of wisdom represented by the cut apple. The lovers therefore embark on this road of self-discovery and seeking, which is both the blessing and the curse of life.

To the right of the man is a flaming tree. Fire is symbolic of his passions and pursuits and the twelve flames represent the twelve houses of the zodiac. The zodiac is a cosmic wheel, ever turning as it brings realizations about life as a constantly moving force. The lovers are beginning to cultivate their five senses and beyond, experiencing the energy of source for the first time.

Symbolic Healing and Guidance

Serpent: spiritual transformation; immortality; duality; life and death.

Jewelry and Body Adornments: self-awareness; sacred; sensual; rites of passage.

Flames: passion; purpose; cleansing; renewal.

The Sun: source; life force.

Upright Message: The Lovers present a unique opportunity to explore cosmic revelations as part of a duo, mirroring, reflecting and unifying, accepting and respecting duality. There is no leader, master or tutor, but rather a meeting of souls who recognize themselves in each other. The card often represents a divine union, a marriage or a relationship deepening on this level. The card can sometimes refer to other relationships on a soul level too, where there is a profound link and meeting of minds. Ultimately, it reflects a mind, body and soul connection. Whenever this card appears in a reading, it presents a choice and usually one that calls for you to stand true in your authenticity. It requires an examination of your values and belief systems.

Reversed Message: There may be some discord in close relationships. Something is a bit out of sync and requires closer examination and nurturing. When the intimacy of the Lovers breaks down it can feel like a small grief or period of confusion. It does not necessarily mean a parting however, but a chance to grow further if addressed mutually. You might see the Lovers move into the Chariot energy and become invincible, exciting and unfettered, or in turn they might have doubts and take a step back to seek counsel with the Hierophant. Things learned now will serve well as a precursor to what we often refer to as "the dark night of the soul." We are still practicing for the ultimate lessons, which we come to bear alone.

VII • The Chariot

Keywords: will; action; momentum; control; determination.
Crystal: Apatite: action; motivation; high energy; moving forward; releasing apathy.

The goddess Freya blazes a trail across the night sky in her mystical chariot. She easily navigates any obstacles in her path, showing mastery of mind over matter by steering with her will and determination alone, rather than the reins before her. The two blue, fabled cats Bygul and Trjegul are both masculine forces often repelling each other and pulling the chariot off course. They represent the opposing forces to be balanced in the universe and pulled back into equilibrium. The cats' coats depict their wild, untamed sides, in contrast to their outward serenity. When the sacred masculine energies work in tandem the momentum is forceful, easy and unstoppable.

Freya's cloak spreads out behind her, displaying an array of animals under the suns and moons. Each one is a reminder of how far she has come and gives strength to put plans into action. The Chariot is about self-determination and how you turn up in the universe to implement your plans and projects.

The idea of the mystical chariot is deeply ingrained in world mythology. It can travel vast distances in the blink of an eye, allowing magical deeds and encounters to happen swiftly and with ease. This card reminds us that we are all in charge of the divine tools at our disposal and that free will is often stronger than fate.

Symbolic Healing and Guidance

Boars: bravery; command; control.

Owls: wisdom; intuition; psychic; telepathy.

Cats: duality; focus; purpose.

Horses: power; freedom; free will.

Crows: transformation; transmuting thought into action.

Suns, Moons, Spirals: duality; day; night; time; cosmos.

Upright Message: The Chariot presents a turning point and a green light to seize the reins and move forward with your plans and desires. You have a strong vision which can be realized externally, and you have the will to see things through. Any obstacles will fall away or can be managed easily with your adaptability and timely adjustments. Be aware it is time to trust and co-create with the universe at great speed. Successful outcomes are ensured if you are prepared to make things happen. Movement forward is imminent and opportunities to travel may also manifest.

Reversed Message: Moving forward with plans may prove difficult just now. Unexpected obstacles may appear. You may be either losing momentum or hurtling too quickly toward an outcome while losing sight of your vision. It is time to pull back and take a deep breath. Be prepared to examine where things do not feel aligned; be flexible and willing to change course. Keep in mind you are the driver and are in control without needing to grip those reins so hard. Anything that appears too difficult may be worth letting go of on the way to your bigger goals.

VIII ✵ Strength

Keywords: compassion; confidence; strength; courage.
Crystal: Tiger's Eye: strength; courage; protection.

The woman lays down beside the lioness and is draped over her form in a soothing and gentle gesture. Although she shows no fear and appears dominant and in control, they are actually equals, and this is the hidden meaning of the card. The nature of all things mirrors our inner worlds at their most wild and beautiful. This unity is where we find incredible strength and compassion.

The lioness is trusting and aware of the intent. The Strength card shows us that we can exert our will while also having compassionate awareness of the world and all her subjects. There is nothing lost or destroyed when we conduct ourselves in this way.

The bees, attracted to the nectar the woman holds, represent the fertility and abundance that can be created through co-existence. Bees often represent our higher selves and soul values. There is an old custom of "telling the bees" when an important event like a birth or death occurs in the family. The bees were thought to carry everything newsworthy across realms, as they are pure of heart and can be trusted with this compassionate role. A tree grows strong in the background and in its bow is a watchful monkey who is resourceful and smart. He embodies the inner strength displayed in this card and the depths of courage we can find within ourselves. Monkey energy also reminds us to do this with a little fun and joy.

Symbolic Healing and Guidance

Lioness: strength; courage; protectiveness.

Bees: integrity; morals; compassion; wisdom.

Monkey: resourceful; influencing; joy;
lightness of being.

Upright Message: The Strength card shows a calm and compassionate approach that will bring the biggest rewards at present. There is a growing inner confidence and awareness of your influence in the world and how it can bring powerful conclusions for good. Your approach is to gently influence and persuade. This is a great time to be an ambassador or leader where your role benefits others. You will have access to a well of inner strength at this time and anything that calls for stamina or quiet persistence will pay off. You should feel very accomplished, for you are learning the fine balance of cause and effect and how mastering your inner worlds makes your environment more harmonious.

Reversed Message: It may be that your inner world is out of sync in this situation. Examine how you are feeling and how it impacts your approach. Is your confidence feeling diminished and vulnerable? This will make you back away from what needs to be addressed. It is okay to feel afraid but don't let your negative inner voice stop you from trying new things or moving forward.

Alternatively, you may be feeling restless, aggressive and angry. It's important to be aware of such feelings so they can be managed. The card can be about taming parts of ourselves that don't serve us so well.

IX ✵ The Hermit

Keywords: introspection; enlightenment; meditation; solitude.
Crystal: Merlinite: magic bringer; psychic visions; shamanism; initiation; nature connections.

The Hermit walks a solitary path to the stone circle nestled at the foot of the hills. The snow-capped peaks rising up in the background show that her wisdom and enlightenment are reaching higher levels. She is alone in the landscape save for the whispering winds and an owl companion who may bring her sustenance and wisdom in the form of visions on this quest for deeper knowing.

The owl carries a key, depicting the secrets that may be unlocked during this time with no distractions from the outer world. The ancient stones surrounding her bring messages from the ancestors of the land and a deeper understanding of spiritual matters from those who have walked the path before.

The Hermit holds in her left hand a staff and a torch, which light the way and bring warmth and illumination to the night. A coppery full moon hangs low in the sky. When the moon is full, the cosmic dance of the sun and moon is in balance, making it a powerful time for ritual and magic to take place. In her hair and on her staff are ribbons embroidered with light language and sacred teachings, which she has channeled and recorded there. The Hermit is drawn to the magical places in the high hills where she can feel the resonance of the land more strongly. It may be that her path is in solitude, but nature and the spirits of the land surround her always. When everything is still, she is ready to receive from divine source. After this period of self-seeking, she will return to the tribe again with great insight and revelations to share.

Symbolic Healing and Guidance

Owl: wisdom; secrets; ancestors.

Standing Stones: ancient wisdom;
connection to the land; nature and the divine;
magic and ritual; pilgrimage.

Torch: illumination; enlightenment; fortitude.

Upright Message: The Hermit has retreated from the world to find peace and solitude in order to strengthen their spiritual practice. While community is the true test in any spiritual journey, in this case there is a lot to be gained from going deep within. Like the Hermit, you will be drawn to take a sabbatical of sorts, a journey away, a retreat or a time of study and introspection. This will likely include a pilgrimage and space to meditate. The links between the earth and the cosmos will ring with deeper meaning when you switch off from the noise of humanity. The very land itself will sing and whisper secrets for you. There is an understanding that when the time is right, you will come back and relay your experiences for the greater good.

Reversed Message: The Hermit may be so happy in their isolation that they retreat too far into themselves and find it hard to return. There is a point in the spiritual journey when it is desirable to do so, so take heed of the cues indicating unhealthy withdrawal. These may include building too many barriers between yourself and loved ones or cutting off communication before cosmic roles have played to completion. Also, in this position the querent might fear being alone so much that it hinders their growth and experience of deeper cosmic lessons and internal revelations.

X · Wheel of Fortune (Fortuna)

Keywords: luck; fortune; fate; karmic wheel; soul contracts.
Crystal: Green Jade: good fortune; abundance; protection; powerful talisman.

Fortuna sets sail on the ever-changing tides. As her boat undulates to and fro, the Wheel of Fortune spins in the background. On the side of the boat are various tools that she may need to steady this voyage. Her boat is deep and watertight but the wheel spins like an eternal compass with no set direction or visible reason. It is governed by things outside our control; just when we think we have a grasp on this universe and its ways, we are confronted by the unseen mechanics and the cogs and wheels that operate beyond our earthly existence.

Hidden behind Fortuna on the wheel itself are Hebrew letters spelling out the name of God. Alternated are the letters Tora(h), the holy Jewish book; spinning in multiple directions it becomes Taro(t), the divination deck; Rota (Latin for wheel); Orat (Latin for speak); and Ator (a version of the goddess deity Hathor). The letters are partially hidden from view here emphasizing this deeper layer of esoterica we have to unravel. The words can be written out as a message: "The wheel of tarot speaks the law of Ator." Thus, we know this movement of the wheel is divine and eternal. It goes back deep in time and forward into our future. Although there is no stopping it, it can be steadied and influenced to make a calmer voyage through life. This is when we start to understand about healing the past to repair the future.

The boat displays a double-headed serpent, which is moving downwards, bringing divine energy into the material world, the intervention of the gods. The dragon in return is rising upwards showing transformation and new knowledge from the lessons learned.

To help Fortuna she has a black cat on board wearing a jade amulet; both are seen as symbols of good fortune. In her collected tools she has various pendulums and potions and a pair of scissors to cut any spent karmic ties or soul contracts. A compass displays the all-seeing eye so she can also be armed with foresight.

Symbolic Healing and Guidance

Serpent: transformation; high and low energies; duality.

Cat: good fortune at sea.

Key: access to hidden knowledge.

Hand: The hand of Fate.

Yahweh and Hathor: divine intervention;
hand of god/dess; eternity.

Upright Message: The fortunes are favorable as you start to realize your blessed role on the wheel and understand the bigger picture, which is constantly playing out. Know that you are a part of it as a contributor and an influencer. By riding the waves you can learn to steady the boat and be prepared for any eventuality. It is a pivotal lesson in both acceptance and responsibility. With this understanding, true miracles can unfold.

Reversed Message: There may be resistance and reluctance to go with the flow. Some events you have struggled with have been kept on repeat for far too long. The good news is there is a glimmer of awareness and the start of a breakthrough. If you often thought "why me?" or that the gods have sent a whole lot of bother your way, then you may just be right. Look for the signs and the deeper meaning; the Fates are only trying to bring your attention to something more profound.

XI • Justice (Ma'at)

Keywords: justice, integrity, truth, law, cosmic order.
Crystal: Sapphire: wisdom, truth and justice.

The divine goddess of justice, truth and cosmic order Ma'at holds up the scales of justice. Anubis has overseen the weighing of the heart ceremony in her halls, and she is ready to declare her findings. On one side of the scales is a human heart and on the other, the stylized feather of truth associated with Thoth and clarity of vision. A lifetime of living well with good values and morality will result in a light heart and safe passage forward. In this story, the passage leads to the afterlife and the eternal, but we can also take this metaphorically to mean: with a pure heart, you can continue on your way without further obstacles. The scales show mirrored versions of Horus in hawk form, representing balance and accountability. Around her neck Ma'at wears amulets and pendulums showing her mastery of divination and ability to see through to the truth of the matter. She also wears a uraeus, symbolizing the goddess Wadjet, a powerful deity of unification and protection. Her ceremonial makeup echoes the eye of Wadjet to show that the truth will be protected.

In this hall and in the darkness of her chambers, the sun god Ra still glitters in attendance. Blooms spring forth showing that the divine beauty of nature is supportive in this process. Nature does not have the luxury of free will, yet it always stands in truth and perfection.

This card serves as a reminder that all actions come with consequences. It speaks to our moral compass and asks us to live within the guidance of the great laws set down in history and interpreted from divine knowledge and commune. It asks us to look at the laws of nature and how we ultimately take responsibility for our choices and accountability for our actions.

Symbolic Healing and Guidance

Hawk: higher wisdom; all-seeing; balance.

Winged Serpent: unification; protection.

Scales: truth and balance.

Upright Message: Justice indicates an examination of values and accountability of actions. If you know you have to make decisions based on the higher good that serves both yourself and others well, then this card indicates that things will work out in your favor. There may be a quest or trial to pass and Justice will look upon your efforts kindly. You may also find yourself in the position to hand out justice and this obligation comes with a great deal of responsibility. If you look inside your heart and pause to consider if your intent is pure, then all actions that follow will move with ease and peace of mind.

Reversed Message: You may be operating from a place of dishonesty or lack of integrity. It may be that you are immersed in fooling yourself about something or trying to stack outcomes in your favor without fully taking into account the consequences. Be aware of taking short cuts, cheats or unwise decisions because it is the easier route. Examine your integrity.

On the other hand, you may be judging yourself too harshly and punishing yourself for unwise decisions in the past. Acknowledge the feelings and perhaps shame associated with this self-criticism and the deeper healing required, so you can release any negative cycles playing out. It is never too late to reset the scales.

XII ✻ The Hanged Man

Keywords: pause; meditation; different perspectives; surrender; acceptance.

Crystal: Howlite: meditation; open-mindedness; letting go; surrender.

The Hanged Man is suspended in an upside-down position. Although strange to fathom, he has put himself in this position intentionally. He wants to see the world from a different perspective and understands that through meditation he can suspend thought, time and current belief systems. On closer examination his demeanor is relaxed, with a bent knee, not tethered, and his arms swing loosely, one toward the ground. The Hanged Man is emptying himself and becoming open to the possibilities of new ideas and perspectives. First, he has to truly surrender and accept that he doesn't have all the answers. This momentary pause on the journey is a sacrifice for the ultimate good and greater revelations to come.

A toad sits in watchful bemusement; his higher energy speaks of change, transformation and enlightenment. He is also a traveler from the Wheel of Fortune vortex just passed, denoting that toads bring good fortune and luck in many cultures. The presence of the toad is endorsing this pause in proceedings as necessary and benevolent. Toadstools grow around the base of the tree, indicating altered states of consciousness, however the tree is strong enough to hold steady. An owl flits in and provides a link to the man through the vines that entwine their way around the scene. The owl also provides a grounding link back to reality from the dark and liminal spaces.

Symbolic Healing and Guidance

Owl: meditation; messages; liminal spaces; edge of night.

Toad: change; magic; transformation; luck;
endorsement; altered states.

Toadstools: altered states; different perceptions; time slips.

Upright Message: The Hanged Man represents an opportunity for change and transformation, but he requires you to pause in proceedings, so you can see more clearly. Try not to get too frustrated if things get stuck or don't go according to plan. The universe is just showing you that you are missing something vital, so you should stop for a bit and go within. Now is the time to let go of perceived outcomes or expected results. The Hanged Man has other ideas and once you get aligned with this flow, things will move and unfold in ways you couldn't imagine. Trust this moment and the new visions you are being gifted with; there will be great value in the dreaming.

Reversed Message: This card reversed is a sign that you are resisting the natural flow and you are rushing into new projects too quickly to take on ideas from others without due consideration. You must build in rest time and a chance to be in the moment, or you might get too run down and be forced to stop regardless of plans. This is the time to slow right down, to exercise self-care and allow meditation and dreamtime to enter your world. Make space for things to unfold without struggle or stress.

XIII Death (The Leveler)

Keywords: endings; beginnings; rebirth; powerful transformation.
Crystal: Black Moonstone: healing; end of suffering; gentle transformation; source.

The figure of Death beckons toward the ferry, ready for the voyage to the underworld. This represents the end of a chapter, the final journey and resolution. It is a short but very intense period you are entering. As you can see in the distance, the journey continues through the pillars high on the hills. This shows transformation and rebirth with new chapters ahead. The pillars also appear in the Moon card and the moon signifies death and the darkness here, while the sun rising signifies life returning and rebirth. The major cards continue, so of course we know this Death card so feared by some is not the end but rather another profound learning experience on the journey.

This is the 13th card in the Major Arcana and displays 13 superstitions surrounding death and dying. They are a reminder of our limited human time and our often illusory perspectives about the mysteries of life and death. There is also a great spiritual equality that arises with this card. Death is the great leveler, which declares all equal. Everyone gets the opportunity to wipe the slate clean and start anew with this card.

Symbolic Healing and Guidance (Thirteen Superstitions)

Falling Feathers: gifts from the angels; spirit.

Coins (Pentacles): to pay the ferryman for a safe passage.

Crow: harbinger of death and symbol of mourning.

Owl: psychopomp and companion in the afterlife.

Red Rose: respect for the deceased.

Death's-Head Moth: death and the dark; transmutation to light.

Pocket Watch: said to stop when the owner dies.

The Bell: an old custom of including a bell in new graves as a means of rescue if the corpse was mistakenly pronounced dead.

Black Cat: healing energies and liminal guide.

Death cap and Amanita mushroom: poison; portal to other realms.

Beetles and the Sun: renewal and rebirth.

Feet Facing the Exit (Skeleton): tradition at a funeral so the dead can't look back.

White Cat: considered a lucky companion; purity; grace.

Upright Message: The Death card is one of the most profound cards in the deck. Its appearance is one to be embraced without fear despite the imagery it shows. Following on from the contemplation that we saw in the Hanged Man, you are now ready to release what no longer serves you and conclude a chapter in your life. You can now take the important lessons learned and make your way to the next chapter. Death can bring powerful transformations and change in its path, so the appearance of the card will be an indication of this especially and also a reassurance that it is okay to close some doors and move forward.

Reversed Message: It may be that the huge changes you are experiencing right now are painful and causing you to struggle against them. You may be hanging onto limiting beliefs or past programming that makes change very difficult. Please be comforted and reassured that the Death card only presents what you need and what will be good for you in the longer term. Hang in there and you will be surprised at what starts to unfold. Seek help if you think you might need some support or new skills in your tool bag to ride out this period. It will be natural to have some sense of loss for the things you used to cling to.

XIV • Temperance

Keywords: balance; guidance; patience; trust; healing.
Crystal: Rose Quartz: unconditional love; self-love; healing.

Temperance is depicted by a winged angelic being. It is sometimes seen as a guardian angel or an ascended guide. In this deck, the presence is channeling the essence of the divine feminine through guidance from Isis, Quan Yin, Brigid and Magdalene.

This card sits serenely between the Death card and the Devil on our journey, somewhat humble and simple in her demeanor, as she carefully transfers energy between her hands. The exchange represents our pure life force, our divine energetic spark, which she holds in balance.

This image may be gentle, but this card holds one of the most valuable lessons about patience and the need for testing and trying, constant adjustments or temperance, until small breakthroughs occur on our spiritual path.

In the distance, the sun shines brightly over the hilltops, mirroring her dazzling halo of gold. A path winds through the hills to the summit, revealing the golden path to attainment, enlightenment and sovereignty. The hill is steep so there is a recognition and acceptance that this will not be an easy journey, but there is a knowing that you are supported and are learning from those who have navigated the path before you.

In this card, temperance is also depicted by the sun melting the snow, the hills becoming pathways, and water and earth blending to foster life. The angel wears the sign of the septenary (a triangle within a square) on her chest, which often represents the seven principles of man and temperance as a gateway to divine healing and the eternal life force of all things. The angel is floating between the earth and the water, a reminder of our alchemical nature. The narcissus heralds rebirth and the snowdrop symbolizes modesty and purity. This card will help you find your truest callings and a return to natural equilibrium.

Symbolic Healing and Guidance

Isis (represented by the abstracted ankh and eye on her forehead): brings beauty and the sacred to all things. Allow yourself to see the world through her eyes.

Quan Yin (represented by the water lily): brings compassion, mercy and forgiveness. Her gifts are truly aligned with this card in that she softens and tempers all actions and beings.

Brigid (represented by her corn cross): brings gifts of protection, wisdom, inspiration and healing. Keeper of the sacred flame and holder of knowledge, she will turn the pages when they are ready to be shown.

Magdalene (represented by the cross and her embodiment of the main figure): brings emotional consciousness, feelings and intuitions. She can show feelings from deep suffering to euphoria and that tempering these emotions can be key to ascension.

Upright Message: You are in an incredibly strong position to channel divine wisdom, which will help you achieve your goals. Remain authentic and take small daily actions rather than sudden giant leaps. This card is about patience, practice, balance and mastering the divine in human form. Know you are supported and not alone.

Reversed Message: A pointer to some imbalance requiring attention and a call to slow down and be more conscious in each moment. You may need to give time over to healing and self-care so you can move into a more peaceful state of being. Focus on the heart center and consider the gentle qualities of Rose Quartz in your realignment and meditations.

XV • The Devil (Mab)

Keywords: addiction; co-dependency; restriction; bondage; dark side; shadow self.
Crystal: Lepidolite: help with addiction and letting go of destructive behaviors.

In the realm of the faeries frequented by witches, the work of the devil was always felt to be near.

Shown here, Mab is queen of this realm, but "she" is also dual in nature and androgynous, representing the balance between male and female, and good and evil. In Scotland, the faeries are often divided into seelie (generally well-meaning unless provoked) and unseelie (those who live in the shadows and plot all manner of wrongdoing when humans wander into their path). Here, two hapless travelers have fallen afoul of an enchantment. They have stepped into a faerie circle where magic is brought forth. They are restrained in a trance, suspended in time and prisoners of their own shadow sides, playing out a loop of destructive behaviors and thoughts in their dreams. They are unconscious and susceptible to influence and persuasion. There are forces that seem far out of reach and out of their control, but actually they are gently wrapped and loosely bound and could get free quite easily if they were to awaken from their slumber. Mab wears bells on her person that can also wake them up at any moment, but she chooses to keep them tethered as long as possible.

Behind the Devil is a scene showing two hills with stone circles, which represent the ideas of good and bad magic. They show that structure and community are the way to gain back control. Eternal fires burn within the two faerie mounds there.

The Devil card asks us to examine our path and our choices carefully, especially when our behaviors become toxic and may do harm to ourselves or others. Although humans are forced to examine the laws of cause and effect, the faeries live outside the usual moral codes.

Symbolic Healing and Guidance

Faerie Ring: spells and bindings that keep someone trapped in bondage.

Faerie Mounds: dwellings of the Tuatha Dé Danann, an ancient faerie race in Ireland; secrets; hidden aspects.

Fire: consumption; pain; purification.

Stone Circles: magic; structure; regaining control.

Upright Message: The Devil card represents your hidden nature and your shadow self. It speaks to our very base earthly desires and how they show up in our lives. Think of the seven deadly sins of pride, greed, lust, envy, gluttony, wrath and sloth; each may manifest in a set of behaviors that are self-destructive. It can often feel like there is a loss of control when these behaviors are led by shadow. We feel helpless and addicted to them. The upright card gives an opportunity to break free from the cycle. It can also point to a period of pleasure and debauchery that is short-lived and relatively safe to explore if shadow is not hiding there.

Reversed Message: Unconscious behaviors and the constant pursuit of pleasure may be presenting problems that need to be addressed. There is a need to shine conscious light on the shadow areas and make friends with them. Make an effort to bring them out of the dark corners and take back control. A breakthrough is coming and when you understand these inner triggers and loops, you will be ready to transcend and free yourself from the bondage of the Devil.

XVI ✼ The Tower

Keywords: change; destruction; chaos; trauma; sudden upheaval.
Crystal: Black Tourmaline: grounding; protection; absorbing negative energies.

Destruction and chaos reign over the scene in the Tower card. Lightning strikes the tower and brings its walls tumbling down. The tower is decorated with statues and effigies from ancient civilizations, showing the severity of this situation. There is no coming back to a familiar place from the events unfolding as the foundations are being destroyed.

The woman in the foreground is lying flat on the ground, clinging to faith. It is all she can do at present to survive and protect herself until things steady and the storm clouds pass. Right now, she is unaware that the bridge is still intact, and the river flows calmly, which will ultimately lead her to safety.

Two crows circle above, often signs of death or endings, but also hope through great transformation and change. Their presence here indicates that order will be restored at some point, just not in the way we expect it. Sparse new flora remains untouched in the foreground ready to reseed and grow stronger.

The Tower card heralds great change that is sudden, intense and all consuming. It can knock us off course and take us unawares, but such events are inevitable in our life, and we are called to surrender to them. Only then can we rebuild and remaster the new beginnings to come.

Symbolic Healing and Guidance

Lightning: destruction; force of nature; transformational energy.

The Tower: chaos and fragmentation.

Cross: faith and hope.

Bridge: safety; escape; guidance.

Statues: loss of knowledge; perceptions; belief systems.

Crows: death and transformation; alchemy.

Upright Message: This card indicates very sudden changes that are difficult and painful to deal with. There will be a sense of great loss and perhaps a period of suffering and readjustment. All indications are that this is a necessary part of your journey now and the difficult events unfolding will bring profound, long-term transformation.

Whatever happens, you still have your faith, purpose and integrity intact. If you let things dissolve and remain as centered as possible throughout this storm, you will emerge stronger and more resilient. There is indeed a way forward and a way to rebuild and start afresh. When we do this, we begin to understand the transformational aspects of change.

Reversed Message: The present trials and tribulations are proving very difficult to handle. You may feel like you are losing control and are being forced to examine everything you held dear or thought to be true. It may be that you will need help or time to readjust to the changes. Building resilience will come again slowly and surely. Just be aware that it is okay to reach out for assistance in getting through this transition.

XVII ☼ The Star

Keywords: renewal; purpose; spirituality; balance; light.
Crystal: Selenite: peace; tranquility; high vibration; emotional healing.

The Star emerges resplendent in the night sky with spirit and grace, and a new purpose. This card depicts a young maiden who is beautiful and pure of heart. She carries with her two vessels. The first is pouring water back into the land to nourish new growth. An abundance of fragrant flowers spring up from the earth, symbolizing fertility and renewal. A solitary bee hovers between the blooms ensuring pollination. The other vessel pours water into five rivulets, which represent the five senses. Once all the senses are activated, joy returns and we are able to relax and experience peace and clarity. We can enjoy living in the moment and developing our skills and sensory gifts further. The ring of six toadstools indicates sensory awareness beyond the five we are commonly aware of.

The main star in the sky radiates seven points of light, which is repeated in the bracelet she wears. The seven rays represent the seven chakras or energy centers in the body. This card indicates a return to earthly and bodily equilibrium as the first step toward renewed spiritual growth and discovery. The Star is coming from a place of innocence, vulnerability and trust represented by the doves. This can often be a powerful time of emotional healing.

Symbolic Healing and Guidance

Butterflies: transformation; grace.

Bee: fertility; abundance.

Water: emotions; senses; healing.

Floral motifs (in the background and on her clothes): growth; renewal.

Doves: peace; gentle; vulnerability.

Star: light; energy; purpose; divine guidance; chakras.

Upright Message: The Star heralds a period of stability and peace. It presents an opportunity for spiritual growth and for manifesting your dreams. It can be a welcome new phase after a period of hardship and will feel exceptionally light and blessed. The universe gently supports you and brings everything into balance again. Life feels easy and you are keen to explore self-improvement and activities that will have a profound effect on your well-being and spiritual path.

Reversed Message: There is a longing for peace and the space to work on spiritual development. You may be feeling out of sorts emotionally after a difficult period in your life and you are finding it hard to see the divine spark in anything. The Star urges you to remain strong and in the light, because those things are always with you and the tiniest of openings can bring them back into view. The peace you seek is within reach so now is the time to look at ways to discover and nurture it.

XVIII ⁕ The Moon

Keywords: subconscious; intuition; psychic ability; feminine wisdom; fears; dreams and nightmares; hidden, illusions.

Crystal: Moonstone: balancing; feminine aspects; calming; centering; psychic and intuitive practices; imagination; creativity.

The Moon looms in the night sky rising up between two pillars, which represent our conscious and unconscious sides. There is a winding path that leads the way to enlightenment, but first we must navigate the deep secrets of the unconscious self. In the sky above the towers hovers a spacecraft on the left and an atom on the right. They represent external and internal mysteries, the vastness of space and its reflection at the atomic level. The Moon is associated with intuition, dreams, mysteries and visions. Here, we learn to separate illusion and deception from reality. At times our fears and anxieties might seem to be heightened as we move closer to the light. The Moon exposes just enough in her glow for us to work with. Beyond the towers is daybreak, clarity and reason; but first the Moon summons the things that reside in the dark.

The woman is flanked by two dogs; one is gentle and placated, taking a drink from the pool, and the other bears its teeth in the start of a grimace, so we are not sure if he means harm or is just fearful. The dogs represent the tamed and wild untethered parts of our mind. The woman is wearing a crescent moon clasp at her throat and also on her crown showing the shifting aspects of the moon, the waxing and waning, and the power of the divine feminine. Two luna moths flying up in the foreground represent the beauty and mystery of the night and the transient nature of all things, as the life of an adult moth is fleeting. A crayfish emerges from the milky pool, indicating the hidden aspects of our being.

Symbolic Healing and Guidance

Luna Moth: transformation; mystery; beauty; transient.

Dogs: opposing aspects; wild and tamed.

Water: emotions; depths; mystery; hidden.

Crayfish: revealing the subconscious; uncovering mysteries.

Towers: subconscious; conscious;
road to enlightenment.

Spaceship and Atom: bringing inner worlds to the
outer realms; mirror aspects.

Upright Message: The Moon appearing in a reading usually means that some aspects are hidden from you right now. There may be parts of your psyche that need to be uncovered or healed in order to unlock some new revelations or mysteries. The card can point to illusions and deceptions that we are weaving in our mind or choosing to ignore. The crayfish is emerging to bring these hidden aspects to the surface now. It may be time to address what is causing you fear and anxiety to clear the path of ascension ahead. The Moon hands over to the Sun each morning and offers new hope and clarity.

Reversed Message: The Moon reversed is wilder and more untamed. Psychic powers and visions may be very pronounced at the moment, with a quickening of signs and synchronicity. This is a very exciting and transformational time with the full power of the Moon showing her hand. However, it can be the most unsettling and confusing too. It is the nature of the universe to hold its secrets close and there will undoubtedly be trickery and deception to navigate at this time.

XIX · The Sun

Keywords: joy; warmth; positive; source energy; youthful; divine masculine.
Crystal: Sunstone: positive energy; masculine aspects; outgoing; vitality.

A child rides a magnificent dragon through the cosmos. Together they bring a positive, joyful energy that is infectious and playful. Very little can hide from the brilliance and warmth of the Sun as it nurtures us and gives life. The Sun shines brightly, representing source, positive energy and all life on Earth. The four suits of the Minor Arcana are represented as fire (the torch), air (the bird), earth (the flowers on her coat) and water (the stems on her coat). These are the building blocks of our alchemical universe and the elements represented in the tarot suits. We are getting ready to apply our wisdom in the real world. The Sun card asks that we go forward with high vibration, vitality and positivity. It also asks that we bring the pure energy of youth and curiosity to our pursuits. The dragon shows we are ready to refine our purpose and take action. It allows us to take up the best qualities of leadership and to run with our ideas and goals. We are a powerful force for motivation when the Sun makes an appearance and the dragon embodies its source energy, winding its way as it breathes fire into everything it touches.

Symbolic Healing and Guidance

Dragon: fire; energy; leadership;
motivation; cosmic energy.

Bird: air; lighthearted; purity; frequency.

Child: purity; joy; curious; love of life.

Sun: source; life source; energy;
divine masculine; action.

Upright Message: The Sun brings in an undeniable sense of joy and happiness. Things will seem easy and success will happen in all areas of your life. This is a time where you attract abundance in all the Minor Arcana areas of creativity, communication, emotional well-being and wealth. Others who share your spirited enjoyment of life will be attracted into your sphere. It is obvious that you are living your best life and this positivity is contagious. The Sun brings the energy of the divine masculine in its purest form, which is light and playful and free from ego. This is a time when you can truly enjoy living in the moment while harnessing the energy of your higher self.

Reversed Message: The Sun reversed represents our inner child and the joy and innocence that we often bury deep down because of our adult responsibilities. This is an indication that your inner child needs to be nourished a lot more. It is time to let that side of you play and explore, to be more joyous and less serious. Once you start following the path of joy, the full brightness of the sun will shine on you again. Remember that the energy of this card is contagious, so making a small effort will start that chain reaction you need right now. If aspects of your inner child need healing then now is a good time to address this.

XX • Judgment

Keywords: judgment; test; absolution; accept; results; graduation.
Crystal: Snowflake Obsidian: learning from experience; protection; banishing; personal growth.

The goddess Pele comes out of her volcanic lair and descends the mountain. Ahead of her she sends her beloved dog, who will seek food and shelter from the people in the village. As a test of their purity and goodness of heart, she will be noting who stops to help this innocent, trusting creature, and who just walks on by. Sometimes she will dress as a beggar and join her faithful friend as they judge the village as a whole and decide if it is worth saving from the lava flow. If the village is deemed to be a kind and welcoming place, then she will reward the people with rich fertile ground, nourished from the very fires and ashes of the earth.

Pele holds up her polished mirror of obsidian to show that any judgment we bestow on others is ultimately a judgment on ourselves. Judgment is one of the most profound lessons in the tarot deck. Once we can fully let go of comparisons and criticism, we can acknowledge that we are all one and there is no separation. It seems so simple a step to walk in the absolution of kindness, but become aware and you will find that judgment is part of our discerning nature, though it may be keeping us from the final steps of enlightenment.

Symbolic Healing and Guidance

Volcano: fire; judgment; wrath; reward.

Dog: kindness; compassion; purity;
innocence; non-judgment.

Obsidian: mirror; soul lessons; awareness;
enlightened path.

Upright Message: The Judgment card appears when you are waking up to your higher states of consciousness. It signals spiritual awakening and a clearing out of any residual processes that are standing in your path. It calls out that "now is the time" to look in the mirror and examine whether or not you are ready. Any karmic stories or embers of shame and regret are ready to be cleared out now. You are evolving into the person you really want to be and choosing how you show up in the world. Compassion, kindness and oneness will be your guides.

Reversed Message: There may be some self-work to do now. You are so close to many breakthroughs and the universe has big plans for you. If you make time for contemplation and meditation, the blocked areas will be revealed. The inner voice and the self-critic might be raising their voices and bringing up those niggling self-doubts. Likewise, you may be projecting those doubts onto others and being unnecessarily harsh and unforgiving in your views. However, this indicates that you are close to a major breakthrough. If you can observe, recognize and understand why these things are playing out and why certain players are appearing to deliver these lessons, then you are halfway there. Things are going to become infinitely more interesting and rewarding.

XXI ☼ The World (Synchronicity)

Keywords: completion; endings; beginnings; success; accomplishment; freedom; travel; expansion.
Crystal: Turquoise: adventure; traveler's companion; protection; unity.

The woman dances through the world, draped in beautiful fabrics from all corners of the globe. Surrounding her are birds representing the different continents. There is an Arctic tern, a bee-eater, a hummingbird, a blue jay, a blue tit, a kookaburra and an African swallow. In turn, each bird holds an amulet crafted by the elders of their lands to bring good fortune and prosperity. All of the seasons are included in this scene, the blooms of spring and summer, the falling leaves of autumn and the delicate snowflakes of winter, showing uniqueness and unity. In her hat, the woman wears a comb, which she can use to propel herself in any direction, past or future.

The high mountains represent how far she has come and the bridge over the river shows the direction of her dance. There is freedom and a sense of adventure awaiting. The completion of one phase is ending and new beginnings are all around. The World signals a completion and a loop to the eternal dance that is life. The appearance of this card signals balance and harmony as well as exciting new opportunities and adventures. There may be a longing to experience more of the world and to connect in different ways; it is time to embrace your wanderlust and curiosity. After a period of growth and learning you are ready to connect and learn firsthand about so many things. The woman is humbled and honored by her surroundings and the many miracles to be discovered.

Symbolic Healing and Guidance

Arctic Tern: travel; migration; tenacity; stamina.

Bee-eater: rainbow; unity; equality; understanding; social.

Hummingbird: joy; happiness; healing; good fortune.

Blue Jay: courage; communication; clarity; curiosity.

Blue Tit: love; loyalty; luck.

Kookaburra: laughter; humor; lightness; joy.

African Swallow: fertility; growth;
abundance; renewal.

Upright Message: Opportunities to expand your horizons open up and you are curious to connect with a diverse range of experiences. Major life markers may present themselves in the areas of unity, love, growth and abundance. Marriages, births, graduations, initiations and career changes may be around the corner. Events occurring now will have great significance in your life. Travel and new experiences are possible. You are very keen to connect on a global level.

Reversed Message: You may require closure or completion of a chapter to move ahead. Big dreams and new beginnings are imminent so now is the time to recognize this. It is time to address any lack of motivation or procrastination. You may be holding back but you are about to enter one of the best phases of your life. Clear the slate and get ready to receive.

Suit of Cups

Ace of Cups (Compassion)

Keywords: compassion; empathy; love; wisdom.
Crystal: Blue Lace Agate: calming, compassion; tranquility; release of emotional blockage.

The woman drinks tea in a fragrant garden, absorbing the purity of her surroundings. Divine gifts of empathy and compassion stream down to her, filling her cup with the wisdom of the intuitive and the psychic empath. She is overcome with gratitude and the knowing that she can help so many people. Tears of deep understanding run down her cheeks. Two blue tits greet her to show their support and love. The Ace of Cups seeks out things of beauty and love in the world and there is an ability to comfort those in need of support and a sympathetic ear. On her sleeve a willowy hare runs toward a protective thistle. The hare represents spirit, and in the ace cards we always find divine gifts and attributes channeled down from spirit. The hare is also associated with Aphrodite, the goddess of love.

Symbolic Healing and Guidance

Element: water.

Qualities: emotions; well-being; health; nurturing; life-giving energy.

Aces: pure potential; beginnings; optimism; divine gifts; passion.

Blue Tits: love; loyalty; joy; luck; divine messengers.

Hare: spirituality; love; mystery; intuition; psychic ability.

Thistle: protection.

Tea: soothing; calm; comfort.

Upright Message: You will have an opportunity to exude love and compassion in your day-to-day dealings or perhaps in a brand new practice. Your experiences will be coming from a heart-centered place, which will help you give and receive freely. Look out for things in your life that stir pure emotion like dance, music and art. There are many roads to helping with compassionate, healing journeys; creativity and self-expression will play a big part.

Reversed Message: In reverse, this card is a call to look after your own emotional well-being. It is an indication that you are giving too much without filling up your own cup. Sometimes it is easy to bury yourself in the worries of others but to be able and ready to help others, you must be in good health and filled with vitality. Your emotions in particular may be out of alignment, either feeling blocked or repressed in some way or too highly tuned and sensitive. Both call for you to address the causes and become more heart-balanced.

Two of Cups (Eternity)

Keywords: love; harmony; partnerships; equality.
Crystal: Lapis Lazuli: truth; wisdom; love; divine communication.

The couple face each other in divine union. They raise their cups in commitment to one another and drink from a deeper level of understanding and communication. They are playing out a ritual dedicated to Isis and Osiris, one of the greatest unions in Egyptian mythology, something that speaks to the eternal universe. The two soulmates are intertwined in love and mutual respect. On their headdresses they display elements of the caduceus as they come together for the first time in fledgling exchange. The serpent shows transformation, and she guards her eggs protectively. The lion signifies fierce passion and desire.

In between the couple, the Nile River flows gently to an oasis, which is calm and abundant. The waters represent deep emotional exchange, fertility and success from this partnership. The woman displays a beautiful white egret on her robes to show she feels calm and at peace in this relationship; there is a spirituality in the union with a meeting of minds and values. The man displays a regal hawk as a mark of respect and gratitude to Horus for overseeing and blessing this union.

Symbolic Healing and Guidance

Element: water.

Qualities: emotions; well-being; health;
nurturing; life-giving.

Twos: balance; comfort; self-control; duality;
yin yang; stop and go; decisions; choices.

Caduceus: healing, union.

Upright Message: The Two of Cups indicates an important new partnership or certainly a deepening of communication between two people. Often this can be a commitment in love or marriage where there is a soul connection. This relationship may have all the ingredients to make the perfect match, which is also balanced and deeply respectful. Alternatively, this could be an important friend or business partner playing a significant part in a new chapter in your life. Trust the flow and the exciting exchanges you may be feeling with this person.

Reversed Message: You may be feeling out of sync in a significant partnership. Misunderstandings or second guessing the other person's feelings or position may come up. There may be more work to do to avoid the relationship breaking down. It is time to examine whether these signs are superficial and temporary or whether they indicate this is not a good match.

Three of Cups (Coven)

Keywords: celebration; friendship; sisterhood; gatherings; harvest.
Crystal: Witches Finger Quartz: positive energy; connectedness; overcoming shadow; white magick.

Three women raise a toast to each other. It is the time of the autumn harvest, and their cups overflow with joy and abundance. They have come together in celebration and friendship, wearing their warmest colors in the chilly autumn air. On their caps they have embroidered emblems of their bounty in bright threads. Each one brings different qualities and skills to the group but together they make the perfect supportive team. Tonight, they will feast, drink and be merry. This sisterhood meets under the stars to put out good intentions and powerful magic into the world around them.

Symbolic Healing and Guidance

Element: water.

Qualities: emotions; well-being; health; nurturing; life-giving.

Threes: balance; solidity; support; divine blessings; consolidation.

Berries and Fungi: harvest; celebration; abundance.

Upright Message: Friendships and bonds are strong right now, so you will benefit from meeting up with kindred spirits to enjoy good company and much laughter. It's time to kick back and enjoy the fruits of your labor. Most importantly, you want to share in a celebration with close friends who have supported the process and made things happen. You are part of a team; everyone is playing an equal role and shares in the bounty and rewards. You know that when this particular group comes together magic will happen. You may be called to join a new circle or start a group for like-minded souls. You are feeding into the connections of the universe around you and want to enjoy and share the energy.

Reversed Message: You may be feeling a lack of connection at the moment. Perhaps you are withdrawing socially after a busy period and just need quiet time. There may have been a lot of celebrations lately that have left you a little worn out around the edges. It is fine to take time for yourself and certainly people will understand and not take offense.

Alternatively, you may have had a period of disconnect or solitude and are now ready to rejoin the social arena. The time spent in withdrawal was purposeful and well spent. Examine friendships and who really has your back; you are in a position to be discerning. Those who truly support you are still around for you when you need them.

Four of Cups (Unfurl)

Keywords: apathy; despondency; contemplation; meditation; choices.
Crystal: Zebra Jasper: removes apathy; provides motivation and determination.

A woman sits under the bow of a tree, deep in her thoughts and meditation. The tree supports her back and the branches provide shade. Four cups sit just to her side offering new opportunities for her to consider. At this time, however, she shows no interest and chooses to ignore them. In her right hand is a fern pressed inside glass, suspended there to indicate she will unfurl in her own time. In her other hand she runs a mala bead string through her fingers. In the night sky a star shines brightly to show that the opportunities will wait and will still be there when she is ready.

At her feet a moth sits waiting for the next phase, and his companion sits by the cups showing potential transformation. Above the woman's head a blue jay makes his presence known. He often prefers his own company, too. Though the jay is usually a noisy bird, he shows his solidarity by adding his quietness to the meditative moment.

Symbolic Healing and Guidance

Element: water.

Qualities: emotions; well-being; health;
nurturing; life-giving.

Fours: robust; solid; strong; complete; stable.

Fern: gentle; unfurling.

Tree: strength.

Moths and Mala: meditation; transformation.

Cups and Star: opportunities; choices.

Upright Message: The Four of Cups brings quiet contemplation and inner work. There are many opportunities presenting themselves to you, but you are right to be discerning and put things on hold for now. Some of these offerings will be amazing and very tempting, but it is not yet the time. Instead, practice the art of saying "no" in order to strengthen your inner resolve. The choices will still be there after you utilize this quiet time to explore meditation and mindfulness. Techniques like this will bring you a great deal of peace and balance. They will eventually open a window of inspiration and motivation again.

Reversed Message: Inner work is the theme of this card. It signals a hiatus, a grand pause, something that you can only do in quiet introspection Although you may be feeling a bit withdrawn, try not to worry too much about it, but rather go with your gut instinct about what you need. If feelings of despondency persist then you may need to seek compassionate help to integrate back into your regular routine.

Five of Cups (Sorrow)

Keywords: sorrow; regret; disappointment; rumination.
Crystal: Malachite: uplifting; mood balancer; release; acceptance.

A woman sits by a riverbank contemplating three goblets that are spilling water onto the earth. Two goblets remain standing, but she is too lost in thought to notice. The banks of the river are covered in forget-me-not flowers, and a single magpie sits with her on an ancient stone, a companion at this sorrowful time. In this scene, there is a focus on disappointment or loss. It may be fleeting but at this time it feels significant and all-consuming.

In the distance, a bridge leads the way to better days and the safety and security of the fortress. A crescent moon hangs low in the sky, offering a welcoming and a period of healing. The Five of Cups shows two cups remaining upright and brings the message that "all is not lost" at the time when you might need it most. The woman wears a pin in her hat depicting a nest with three eggs, showing hidden potential in the situation. On the ground beside the upright cups is a little goddess pendant, which is protective and nurturing, providing comfort and condolence.

Symbolic Healing and Guidance

Element: water.

Qualities: emotions; well-being; health; nurturing; life-giving.

Fives: conflict; discord; miscommunication.

Magpie: one for sorrow from the folk poem.

River: emotions.

Goddess Amulet: comfort.

Nest and Eggs: potential just out of sight.

Upright Message: A situation of loss or great disappointment is upon you. It can be physically felt and very tangible or also emotionally led. The cups show our emotional balance here, mostly drained and depleted but with some reserves standing strong. Although these occurrences are being felt very strongly and you may be in the midst of sorrow and regret about how things have played out, there is every indication that things will improve in the near future. The forget-me-nots gradually stir good memories, or the important lessons learned, and then lead you to a happier, more secure place and peace of mind.

Reversed Message: The message is about addressing regrets and coming to peace with things that cannot be undone. Sometimes, it is possible to accept and move on naturally by yourself. In this instance, you might have to share your burden and open up about how you are feeling. Others can reassure you and help you release and move on eventually.

Six of Cups (Joy)

Keywords: reminiscing; childhood; sentimentality.
Crystal: Amber: memory; past life recall; healing; joy.

Two sisters exchange gifts in front of their childhood home. Six vessels containing blooms brighten the path all around the door, and little heirloom jewels sparkle in their clothes. This reunion brings happy memories and lots of warm tales to share. Two magpies flit into view, a symbol of joy and comfortable companionship. Smoke billows from the chimney. Later, they will sit by the fire reminiscing about their childhood experiences and sharing family lore. The ancestors will draw around the hearth and be part of the scene, just as real as the cat who slips in quietly to listen.

The Six of Cups brings happy sentiments and encourages us to look back on the experiences that made us who we are.

Symbolic Healing and Guidance

Element: water.

Qualities: emotions; well-being; health; nurturing; life-giving.

Sixes: abundance; balance; stability.

Magpies: two for joy from the folk poem.

Smoke and Hearth: ancestors; family.

Heirloom Jewels: memories; sentiment, nostalgia.

Cat: familiar; comfort.

Upright Message: There is an opportunity to take a stroll down memory lane. A particular place and time may be tugging at your heartstrings and stirring up emotions. You will enjoy reminiscing and revisiting this time especially if you can share the memory with others. Perhaps the feelings are enhanced by engaging all your senses, which might involve looking at old photo albums, handling heirlooms, or collecting vintage or nostalgic items that remind you of childhood.

Alternatively, your heritage and ancestors may be calling you to explore their lives and traditions.

Reversed Message: You could be getting a little obsessive about the past. Reliving memories and recalling good times is bringing you pleasure, but there is a tendency to want to stay there too long. You start to think that things were so much better in the past and find unfavorable comparisons to the present day-to-day. It's time to examine what holds you there and why it is preventing you from making wonderful new experiences and memories in the present. Are you looking through rose-tinted glasses? Are you fearful of leaving cherished memories behind? Perhaps you feel guilty about truly living your life in the moment. The Six of Cups asks you to let your inner child back in and bring them with you. It's time to let loose and have a little fun with your feet planted firmly in the here and now.

Seven of Cups (The Conjurer)

Keywords: choices; opportunities; desires; illusions; smoke and mirrors.
Crystal: Azurite: decision-making; focus; manifestation.

The conjurer emerges from the dark cosmic realms of no-thing. Stars begin to twinkle into view as she awakes from her trance. Surrounding her is a strange assortment of items and beings emerging from seven ritual vessels. They float into the physical realm on clouds and represent her thoughts and desires. All of the items are gifts from the universe brought into being by her will. Some bring dual meanings and hard lessons, while others are more pleasant. The conjurer wears a scrying mirror for looking into and reflecting back out to the viewer. This theme is mirrored in the Judgment card, with the Seven of Cups representing choices and also judgments.

The shrouded figure represents the need for illumination and spiritual growth, or a desire to look into the afterlife. The flip side can be over-reliance on belief systems. The heart represents love, intimacy, connection, and human compatibility; emotions that can flip to painful experiences quite quickly.

The tower mirrors the Major Arcana card and can signify chasing power, success and strength. We know from the Tower card that it can come tumbling down. The intact tower here gives choices on how such events may unfold. The wreath or berry plant depicted is about growth, honor and status, perhaps through education or birthright. There is a level of pride or entitlement to look out for in the dual aspect. The crystals, coins and jewels are about wealth and how you approach their accumulation. The dragon here is indicating the Christian notion of the supernatural being a dangerous pursuit. Dragons are very powerful and magical but everything in the cups has dual meanings depending on the viewer's perception or how they use them. The snake is passion itself and hidden knowledge. The flip side may be fear and betrayal.

Symbolic Healing and Guidance

Element: water.

Qualities: emotions; well-being; health;
nurturing; life-giving.

Sevens: obstacles; challenges.

Shrouded Figure: afterlife; mystery; the unknown.

Heart: contact; compatibility.

Tower: stability; strength; success.

Wreath: honor; status; pride.

Crystals and Coins: wealth; prosperity; comfort.

Dragon: power; magic; danger.

Snake: passion; secrets; sexual energy.

Upright Message: The Seven of Cups is a very powerful manifestation card. It is exploring our deepest dreams and desires and presenting them back to ourselves. Often this provides choices and indeed moral dilemmas. It is no accident that the manifestations can also represent the seven deadly sins and a deeper reflection on ego. The conjurer/shaman has to be pure of mind to assist in such magic. Now you are being asked to carefully consider all possible outcomes and make good choices.

Reversed Message: You may be feeling overwhelmed by choices and acting from a place slightly skewed by ego. Reflect on your root values and their dual aspects such as: honor/pride, passion/lust, power/wrath, beliefs/sloth (or lazy thinking), love/envy, wealth/gluttony, success/greed. Sometimes, these may be interchangeable depending on the situation and the shadow side of things. Be careful what you wish for.

Eight of Cups (The Trailblazer)

Keywords: departing; dejected; seeking; alone.
Crystal: Green Aventurine: soothes and heals; brings luck and good fortune; helps transitions.

The woman is turning her back on a table where eight teacups stand stacked and empty. They are conspicuous in their arrangement and the gap between them suggests feelings of something missing. The people from the tea party have departed and now the woman is alone. There is nothing to keep her here and part of her feels dejected and abandoned, yet she knows this has come about because of her will. With a final look back, she embarks on her new journey, which will require some healing and nurturing. The hilltops before her are barren, blank canvases meaning there is a desire to seek out the new and build from the ground up. The woman knows she may have to leave rich floral pastures behind her and take a leap of faith. This road will not be easy and there may be elements of escapism or avoidance of unresolved issues.

Her coat is embroidered with a large dragonfly symbolizing change, transformation, spiritual growth and the emotional maturity that is not quite there yet. Her long braid shows tales and entanglements behind her. She has woven it fresh and neat to symbolize the new stories ahead. A comb bearing a small carved crow is tucked in her hat facing forward as a reminder not to be afraid of change.

In the familiar landscape, a galloping chalk horse comes into view. Little does she know that her experiences here have taught her about freedom, independence and self-autonomy. The tree indicates strength and endurance for the journey ahead. It may not be apparent yet, but this woman is starting a journey of transmutation out of the embers of things lost and friendships expired. If she looks up, she will notice a comet tearing across the night sky toward an unknown destination, blazing a trail of new beginnings and potential.

Symbolic Healing and Guidance

Element: water.

Qualities: emotions; well-being; health; nurturing; life-giving.

Eights: strength; prosperity; infinite success.

Dragonfly: transformation; change; spiritual growth; maturity.

Crow: overcoming fear of change.

Braid: new stories to be told.

Comet: trailblazer; wayshower.

Horse: freedom; independence; autonomy.

Upright Message: The Eight of Cups indicates a decision has been made and you need to walk away from a place or situation for your own well-being. Your departure is led by feelings of dejection, dissatisfaction or emptiness. You may be aware that it's a "giving up" situation rather than a "fighting on" one and that you have no choice because there simply is no energy left to continue. This is acceptable and right for you at present. Despite the road not being the easiest, there are good things ahead including a chance to mature and find your authentic self. In some ways, the solitary path is the path of the trailblazer and wayshower.

Reversed Message: The decision to stay or go may be wearing hard on you right now. Go within to find the desires of your heart and what you truly want from life. You may find that things are not aligned, and you really do wish to move on, or it may be that something is worth holding on for. Be aware that you do have wells of strength and maturity to try and make the situation better if you choose to stay, but it will take time and effort on your part.

Nine of Cups (The Wishmaker)

Keywords: contentment; satisfaction; enjoyment.
Crystal: Amazonite: calm; well-being; positivity; the law of attraction.

The woman is sitting at her stall, happy, warm and content with life. She sips a soothing blend of herbal tea from a handmade ceramic cup. Behind her are eight more cups from her potter's wheel to be sold or traded. Each cup is unique, and she has poured love and care into their creation, finding fun in adding little emblems of luck and joy. A cat companion is curled up on her lap, trusting her calming energy.

The woman has a sunny disposition and is happy to chat and exchange greetings at leisure with the folks that stroll by. Occasionally, they purchase a cup and stay a while to sip tea. There is a great deal of enjoyment and satisfaction in this scene. Scarcity has no place here and the woman knows that she is a powerful manifester who will be provided for with little effort. Indeed, she takes great pleasure in her work and sees it as an extension of her soul's purpose.

The Nine of Cups represents a time of positivity and enjoying one's achievements. Everything feels perfectly aligned. The beautiful toadstools in the foreground make you wonder about the magic and blessings of the universe. It is easy to do so from this perspective and you will want to indulge in pleasures, small indulgences and beauty.

Symbolic Healing and Guidance

Element: water.

Qualities: emotions; well-being; health; nurturing; life-giving.

Nines: inner strength; big life lessons; enlightenment.

Cat: contentment; harmony; satisfaction.

Ladybird: luck; blessings; attraction.

Sunflower: enjoyment; abundance.

Toadstools: magic.

Upright Message: The Nine of Cups invites you to pause a while and enjoy all the wonders you have created. It is a card of gratitude and intense enjoyment, so make sure you savor it all and indulge in the moment. This card is often referred to as the "wishmaker," and is an indicator of good fortune. There is something powerful in the saying that "wealth attracts more wealth." You feel on a bit of a roll but relaxed and supported at the same time.

Reversed Message: Even while everything seems perfect on the outside, there might be lingering discomfort, disbelief or self-doubt inside. Even in the best of times is there a niggling worry that things are too good to be true? Go within and find the roots of this unease. Find the things that need to heal deep in the shadow self and confront the fear that rises up when times are especially good. Use this opportunity well.

Ten of Cups (The Lightbearers)

Keywords: love; relationships; unity; harmony.
Crystal: Morganite: love; strengthens relationships; cooperation; harmony.

A couple approach an idyllic domestic scene with a beautiful cottage nestled beside a strong, ancient tree. They each carry a lantern and in the boughs of the tree eight more cupped lanterns illuminate the way. Two children laugh and play in the yard; the atmosphere is joyful and filled with love. The cottage is secured by a stone wall and a gate. A contented cat watches from the garden wall, and nearby is a wishing well.

The Ten of Cups is concerned with relationships, love, unity, family and friends. The couple has achieved divine union along with the comfort and harmony that comes with truly being in step with loved ones. The card speaks of harmony, security and fulfillment of your wishes and dreams.

Symbolic Healing and Guidance

Element: water.

Qualities: emotions; well-being; health; nurturing; life-giving.

Tens: completion; accomplishment; fulfillment.

Cat: contentment; harmony; satisfaction.

Wishing Well: dreams coming true.

Lanterns: illumination; divine guides.

Upright Message: There is a sense of completion and contentment with this card. You are at peace with yourself and your life. Having explored your authentic self and resolved various challenges and experiences, you are ready for new life chapters and a calmer existence. Reaching this place has allowed you to enjoy life and share your joy with others. The simple things and the quiet oneness with all things will attract you and reward you. You are open to new and wonderful relationships if you have not already found them.

Ideal love partners may appear, or existing unions may be strengthened. There may be commitments and moving to the next level, for example, moving house, having children, or undertaking new projects together. Deep friendships and family bonds surround you and protect you at this time. There is much to celebrate.

Reversed Message: You may be considering your relationships right now and the hopes and dreams you had for them. Perhaps everything did not go perfectly according to your plan or vision. You know you are happy, and these relationships are worth it, but you may be internalizing about how things could be improved. Once you have more clarity, you will be able to discuss and communicate your thoughts and feelings. Examine your needs and expectations, but also where you might have dropped the ball and what you can work on more. Timing is important, so don't go rushing in on the defensive until you can see the whole picture with empathy and no blaming or shaming.

Page of Cups (The Tea Leaf Reader)

Keywords: intuitions; psychic ability; study; service; uncovering knowledge.
Crystal: Celestite: connection to the divine; messages; dreams; intuitions.

The Page of Cups works in the intuitive realms. Messages from the divine are very tangible and well within reach. Creative ideas come with spontaneity and intuitive thoughts can be read with clarity. The page stands in a beautiful opulent garden by the shore. The waters beyond are still and calm with a small island just off in the distance. The landscape indicates a growing mastery of hidden gifts and psychic abilities. In the page's hand is a teacup used for tasseomancy (tea leaf reading). It is one of her new studies and additions to her divination repertoire. Other paraphernalia hangs within reach around her neck, including a tea strainer and pouch with loose Earl Grey. The intent with this page is to be of service and she is ready to explore her gifts and give counsel on her travels. As an additional benefit to her deepening perception, many surprising and creative ideas are discovered. These are indicated by the presence of the flying fish manifesting from her cup. The page is full of wonder and curiosity at her blossoming gifts.

Symbolic Healing and Guidance

Element: water.

Qualities: emotions; well-being; health;
nurturing; life-giving.

Pages: apprentice; potential;
creativity energy.

Tasseomancy Cup: divination;
intuition; psychic gifts.

Island: inner self.

Flying Fish: surprise; the unexpected;
curiosity; wonder.

Upright Message: You are developing skills and uncovering new aspects of yourself. You might be drawn to the magical arts of divination and healing. Counsel and the ability to help others will be important to you and a motivation for expanding on your psychic gifts. You have all the tools you need at your disposal and divine gifts can be channeled successfully. Be open and curious to the unexpected and surprises when you embark on this journey, about yourself and others. Perception needs to be flexible; beliefs suspended. The card often heralds good news from the emotional realm, major life events and reasons to celebrate.

Reversed Message: You are being asked to develop maturity on this path because it is a serious one, weighty with responsibility. Watch your confidentiality, delivery manner and disclosure, all things that come with experience and maturity. You are extremely gifted and everything feels so exciting but stay humble and balanced. Check in with your ego and motivations at each stage of your development.

Knight of Cups (The Kelpie Keeper)

Keywords: charming; intuitive; diplomatic; fluid.
Crystal: Ocean Jasper: balance; gentle; intuitive; safe travels.

The Knight of Cups rides a kelpie steed into the waves. This knight is deep thinking, emotive and romantic. His helmet and clothing display fish (emotions), shells (safe travels), coral (creativity), and pearls (wisdom). A shoal of fish swirl in a circular motion under the knight's robes, showing a fluid nature at one with the surroundings. The kelpie steed wears reins and ribbons bearing joined hearts, representing romanticism. From its mane, a plume displays more fish, indicating imagination and creative thoughts. Two seahorses lead the way: these "knights of the sea" are considered to be lucky. This calm, reassured, and charming knight has a tendency to go with the flow.

Symbolic Healing and Guidance

Element: water.

Qualities: emotions; well-being; health; nurturing; life-giving.

Knights: action; vitality; service; honor.

Kelpie: shapeshifter; fluid; liminal.

Fish: creative expression; emotions.

Hearts: romance; love; beauty; charm.

Seahorses: courage; adventure; luck.

Shells: travel; protection.

Coral: creativity; vitality.

Pearls: wisdom; beauty; treasures.

Upright Message: The Knight of Cups brings in creativity and compassion. You may be feeling a call to travel and help others. Expect opportunities to exercise diplomacy or use your charisma and charm to get things done. Serving community or humanitarian missions might be in the cards. Your strengths will lie in keeping a calm and relaxed approach while moving forward. Remember to be flexible and move with the tides and the natural flow of life. This knight can also be the bearer of good news.

Reversed Message: Be careful of being ruled by your emotions or jumping to conclusions too quickly. The message of this card is to slow down, consider and communicate. The shoal of fish can grow larger and larger but if they stick together and hold steady, they remain in harmony. In the reversed position, you are called not to judge a situation or person too quickly. Your perceptions could be fallible on occasion, so look out for being swept along by a current of thought without the facts.

Queen of Cups (The Coral Queen)

Keywords: psychic; emotional realms; mysteries; liminal spaces; divine knowledge.
Crystal: Larimar: high vibration; healing; balancing; divine connections.

The Queen of Cups sits serenely on her throne, situated at the place where the land meets the sea. She occupies the subconscious mind and the liminal spaces, holding many mysteries yet to be shared with others. The sea and the sky are calm and centered like this queen who exudes tranquility and peace of mind.

Her robes and her throne blend into one and are richly decorated with jewels, fish and other sea life. In her hand is a closed chalice representing her secrets and knowledge. It is decorated with angel wings to show that her wisdom comes from divine sources, and dolphins, which are considered to be deeply empathic and compassionate creatures. This is a fair ruler who balances intellect and emotions. She is also highly in tune with the spirit realms and protects many mysteries.

Symbolic Healing and Guidance

Element: water.

Qualities: emotions; well-being; health; nurturing; life-giving.

Queens: feminine; mature; nurturing; ruler.

Fish: creative expression; emotions.

Hearts: romance; love; beauty; charm.

Seahorses: courage; adventure; luck.

Shells: travel; protection.

Coral: creativity; vitality.

Pearls: wisdom; beauty; treasures.

Dolphins: empathy; compassion.

Covered Chalice: mysteries; esoteric knowledge.

Wings: messages; angels; higher realms;
divine knowledge.

Upright Message: This queen with all of her compassion and wisdom indicates a powerful, nurturing force in your life. You may be entering initiation with a mature female presence and master of the magical arts. You in turn may be called to strengthen your own knowledge and teach others. There may be a student to take under your wing, or a group to lead into deeper practice.

Reversed Message: Be aware of being led by emotions or getting in too deep with others as there may be some illusion and hidden aspects involved. A good measure of intellect may be required to unravel what is real. Imagination and visualization are powerful forces in this card. Be sure to ask continually what is real and what can be trusted?

King of Cups (King of the Sea)

Keywords: compassionate; balanced; kind; fair.
Crystal: Caribbean Calcite: emotional intelligence; spaciousness; relaxed; balance; flow.

The King of Cups sits comfortably on his throne overseeing his domain on land and sea. He is a balanced ruler, fair and kind, and there is a level of emotional maturity in all his dealings. He holds a goblet close to his chest, suggesting open emotions kept in check. In his other hand, he holds a shell scepter in a relaxed manner, showing his power but also his ability to listen with compassion. On his belt, he has three charms: a fish to show his creativity and ability to express himself, a crystal to show his wealth of knowledge, and a pouch to show the mysteries of the sea and human emotions. In his robes and crown there is a wealth of shells and coral, with more fish gently going about their day. Two dolphins leap suddenly out of the choppy waves near the shore, yet the king remains calm and collected when presented by this sudden surprise. The sea gives way to a calm vista and the royal moored ship, which can be used at any time to survey the kingdom and meet its inhabitants. A lighthouse represents the further community and the hope they feel under this leader. The people are happy and secure with the King of Cups in power.

Symbolic Healing and Guidance

Element: water.

Qualities: emotions; well-being; health; nurturing; life-giving.

Kings: masculine; mature; generous; ruler.

Fish: creative expression; emotions.

Shells: travel; protection; listening; compassion.

Coral: creativity; vitality.

Pearls: wisdom; beauty; treasures.

Dolphins: empathy; compassion; curious; surprises.

Crystal: wealth; wisdom.

Lighthouse: community; protection; hope.

Ship: freedom; power; connections.

Upright Message: This king rules fairly and with compassion. He represents a mature and balancing force within your life, perhaps a mentor or advocate who can provide emotional support and encouragement. You may be called to reach out and nurture some growing talent yourself. If you feel this would be the right thing to do, it will be a rewarding time for you.

Reversed Message: This king is a master of his emotions; he serves and protects very easily without depleting himself. When the card is reversed it is asking you to check in on your emotional reserves and make sure your boundaries are strong. It may be that you are trying to be all things to all people without fully balancing those aspects of yourself.

Suit of Pentacles

Ace of Pentacles (The Investor)

Keywords: new opportunity; investment; growth; generosity; altruism.
Crystal: Stitchtite: helps attract abundance; coaches in wealth management; balanced approach to money.

A man stands in an abundant garden. A column of energy from the heavens delivers a pentacle, representing divine gifts around money and wealth. A lush hedge is fashioned into a gateway to show that this is a portal card. Whenever this ace appears he has the ability to move in any direction through the deck or reading to initiate new opportunities and good fortune. He is pointing to the infinite possibilities and gifts of the universe being within reach; this message is echoed by the presence of the ouroboros surrounding the pentacle.

In the distance, mountains rise up to dizzying heights and the man stands firm and stable against a tree. On his person, he wears rich finery and various emblems of prosperity. Lilies represent fresh life and fertility. There is a bee on his hat for wisdom, diligence and accumulation. In his cowl, a dragon guards a pearl, showing protection, investment and nurturing. A joyful elephant decorates his coat for good luck and stability. Finally, he wears a crane on his sleeve for everlasting abundance and the cyclic nature of all things.

Symbolic Healing and Guidance

Element: earth.

Qualities: security; stability; wealth; investment; the material realm.

Aces: pure potential; beginnings; optimism; divine gifts; passion.

Portal: movement; security; freedom.

Lilies: new life; purity; fertility.

Bee: wisdom; accumulation.

Dragon: protection; nurturing; investment.

Elephant: good fortune; stability.

Crane: everlasting; duration; cyclic.

Upright Message: The Ace of Pentacles is a great card to receive when starting a new project or business. It's a reassurance that your investment will be rewarded. You may have nurtured something with time, money and energy. The seeds have been planted and this is the beginning of a successful and rewarding journey in the material realm. Aces bring in the energy of the divine, so there will be beautiful harmony and balance in your growth at this time. You will feel truly blessed.

Reversed Message: In reverse, this card can indicate a slight delay in material rewards. Remember, the ace is a seed card, handing you the divine gifts to plant in fertile soil. Be patient because what you are nurturing right now will have far-reaching effects into the future. Some seeds may not take or be scattered to the winds, but this card is also a portal to a new cycle, so pay close attention. Nothing you are doing right now will be a wasted effort.

Two of Pentacles (Comfort and Joy)

Keywords: adaptable; energetic; flow; multi-tasking.
Crystal: Boji Stones: balance; measure; yin yang.

A woman sweeps through a lush and vibrant landscape. She is flanked by two strong trees showing balance and stability. Ahead of her, two firebirds fly in unity, one flitting ahead and then the other, in an infinite loop moving forward. The birds carry in their beaks two pentacles, showing that there are two things to manage and juggle in this woman's busy life. She strides forward purposefully, using a walking stick to steady herself while she moves through the dense forest.

Her cloaks and accessories are embroidered and luxurious, showing success, achievement and purpose. On her satchel is a grasshopper, an emblem of luck, prosperity and wisdom. The woman is striding out into the world to seek her fortunes. It is possible that she may be managing a career or business of her own, and she is likely to be balancing this with other commitments like home and family life, friends and relationships. Several small butterflies rise up from the forest floor to indicate a very busy and transformative time.

Symbolic Healing and Guidance

Element: earth.

Qualities: security; stability; wealth; investment; the material realm.

Twos: balance; comfort; self-control; duality; yin yang; stop and go; decisions; choices.

Firebirds: movement; progress; energy; alchemy.

Trees: solid; stable; support.

Grasshopper: wisdom; good fortune.

Upright Message: The Two of Pentacles indicates you have a lot on your plate right now. This is good and exciting, you feel fulfilled. All parts of your life are very rewarding and your days are busy. Give gratitude for your health and ability to manage everything you have created. Remember to take rest breaks and pauses to re-plan or celebrate. All those little things that keep you organized and functioning comfortably can be bumped up your priority list. Make sure to leave time for joyous moments, to ensure the balance stays in check and your day well oiled.

Reversed Message: You may be overstretched and overbooked. Things are beginning to pile up despite your usual coping mechanisms. It is time to dust off the to-do list and bring some planning and structure back. Sort out the backbone of your business or practice so you can enjoy the rest. Do it in small bite-sized pieces and don't neglect your self-care and breathing space; plan that on the calendar first and foremost.

Three of Pentacles (Harmony)

Keywords: teamwork; harmony; cooperation; sharing.
Crystal: Super Seven: divine connections; greater good; cooperation; unity; oneness.

In a scene reminiscent of the famous poem "The Owl and the Pussycat," a woman shares space in the wilderness with an owl and a cat. These two may be strange bedfellows, but they illustrate the uniqueness in each of us and the diversity we create when we come together as a team.

Each person plays a particular role and has a unique skill to contribute. Looking down on proceedings from a higher perspective, the owl represents knowledge, expertise and discernment. The cat is focused, alert and ready for action. The woman in turn provides the plan and keeps the project on course. Sometimes she manages to do so and sometimes not. Occasionally, they swap roles, but the most important thing is that they work together. They each carry a pentacle around their neck as a symbol of their commitment to their joint project. The lilies surrounding the scene represent harmony and pure intentions.

Symbolic Healing and Guidance

Element: earth.

Qualities: security; stability; wealth; investment; the material realm.

Threes: balance; solidity; support; divine blessings; consolidation.

Owl: wisdom; oversight.

Cat: intent; implementation.

Woman: guide; nurture; birthing ideas.

Lilies: pure; inspiration; harmony.

Upright Message: The Three of Pentacles is concerned with teamwork, community and cooperation. You recognize that your latest project requires a diversity of skills to bring it to life. You may need to hand things over to someone's greater expertise and consult with them to get things done. This card recognizes the value in this process and also the importance of each person's contribution and vocation.

Reversed Message: Watch out for unease or lack of harmony in a team. Is someone trying to act superior and give out orders? Who is feeling undervalued or unappreciated? If there are some unresolved tensions or misunderstandings, work can come to a standstill if the air is not cleared. This card is an indicator that someone needs to gently mediate and ensure everyone feels good about their role.

Four of Pentacles (Blackbird Garden)

Keywords: accumulate; covet; hoard; save.
Crystal: Ametrine: balance; clearing blocks; healing; attracting abundance.

A woman sits alone in a colorful garden. Surrounding her, four blackbirds are collecting four pentacle charms. The charms feature the all-seeing eye, showing how carefully she guards her treasure. There may be feelings of mistrust or concern that things may be taken from you. Blackbirds are associated with mystery and the balance of night and day. They remind us of our duality and to be mindful of our shadow selves. In nature, blackbirds will covet food and often in our gardens they will dominate the bird feeders if given the chance. We might also witness them quickly stripping a bush of its berries before we've had a chance to gather any of the bounty.

Like her avian companions this woman is happiest accumulating her bounty and riches. It can be her main focus and gives her enjoyment. We can think of her as a bit of a hoarder or obsessed with the accumulation of all things precious and beautiful. There is value in developing the skills of resourcefulness or negotiation. However, she is not good at sharing and may be very selfish in her pursuit of wealth.

Symbolic Healing and Guidance

Element: earth.

Qualities: security; stability; wealth;
investment; the material realm.

Fours: robust; solid; strong;
complete; stable.

Blackbirds: forward; resourceful; successful.

Wand: manifestation.

Trees: protection.

Moon: mystery; coveting.

Upright Message: The Four of Pentacles asks you to examine your feelings around wealth and money. You feel very gratified and buoyant right now, but something about your approach and attitude may start to bother you. Look into the deep emotive side of your apparent success. Does it stress you out that you may lose your security or wealth? Are old feelings of scarcity making you miserly and afraid to share or spend? Perhaps there are past experiences that have made you distrustful of people's intentions around your gains.

It is a good time to examine the shadow thoughts and strive to become more at ease with your money relationships. Trust the ebb and flow and have faith that the universe will take care of your needs. By all means, save for a rainy day and be responsible, but bring back in the balance, joy and generosity of having and sharing.

Reversed Message: The reversed message is just the same, but you have an awareness that it is making you unhappy and unhealthy. Perhaps you have replaced everything meaningful in the pursuit of money and feel empty about your acquisitions. Or, maybe you've just been very thoughtless in your collecting and saving with no satisfaction. In any case, it is time for a change.

Five of Pentacles (Aurora)

Keywords: loss; abandonment; poverty; isolation.
Crystal: Labradorite: stress relief; divine protection; aura protection; positive energy.

In one of the stories of the goddess Sedna she is a shunned, young orphan girl. The villagers arrange to take her out to sea and throw her to the waves to drown. In the tragic tale she clings to the side of the kayak and her fingers are chopped off, hurtling her into the deep. Sedna is then transformed into a great creatrix being, mother of the sea. Her severed fingers become the various creatures who live in the sea and on the nearby land.

The Five of Pentacles depicts the uneasy and brutal realities of poverty, loss, isolation and banishment. Our main figure is out in the cold, she is alone in an icy arctic scene with minimal possessions. In her hands she holds a large piece of magical labradorite that appears to capture the aurora borealis, a sign of heavenly protection. Around her is a gathering of spirit animals holding pentacle charms, each one bearing a specific gift and healing message of hope.

The girl feels abandoned and alone; she may have lost touch with her support systems and is going through a hard time. She is finding it very hard to remain positive and cannot see the possibilities of help that are being gifted to her, even in this cold place. In the far distance beyond the tundra is a line of evergreens that indicate the future is brighter. On her back are the wings of a thunderbird, showing the potential to reinvent oneself and soar again.

Symbolic Healing and Guidance

Element: earth.

Qualities: security; stability; wealth; investment; the material realm.

Fives: conflict; discord; miscommunication.

Labradorite: protection; healing; hope.

Aurora Borealis: sacred gifts; divine help.

Tundra: barren; cold; unforgiving.

Thunderbird: reinvent; rise up; transform.

Crow: intuition; transformation.

Polar Bears: strength; survival.

Salmon: effort, determination.

Arctic Fox: trust; community.

Upright Message: You may have had a sudden misfortune or financial crisis. You are feeling the effects but also the sting of having to go it alone. You may feel you can't ask for help or that friends have abandoned you in your hour of need. This too shall pass, and you will become aware of the help and resources still available to you.

Reversed Message: A difficult financial hardship may be coming to an end; change and good news is around the corner. However, in this reversed position, we are asked to consider the deeper lessons learned from poverty and hardship. How has the incident changed you and can you make a difference in the lives of others? Did you feel hardened by the lack of help or more determined to reach out to someone in need in the future?

Six of Pentacles (Six for Gold)

Keywords: generosity; sharing; distribution; charity.
Crystal: Fire Agate: powerful protection; deflection; mirror; vitality; kindness.

A woman is enjoying a beautiful garden. She is dressed in fine clothes and opulent jewels. Her jacket is decorated with the moon and stars to indicate she is blessed and the universe has her back. On her capulet and crown is a vibrant sun, showing wealth, abundance and vitality. The woman knows she is very fortunate and is keen to give something back. Beautiful fire agates glitter in her jewels reflecting how she sends her generosity out into the world.

The woman has tossed six pentacle coins into the air, and they are caught by six watchful magpies, a symbol of gold and riches. This scene shows fair distribution; each bird receives a coin, which the woman is in a good position to give.

The Six of Pentacles shows the positive flow of wealth, illustrating that if we help others when we are able to, then we will also be aided if we are in need. The give and take balance is echoed in nature and our universal cycles. Bestowing gifts on others makes us richer in ways money can't buy.

Symbolic Healing and Guidance

Element: earth.

Qualities: security; stability; wealth; investment; the material realm.

Sixes: abundance; balance; stability.

Magpies: six for gold; wealth; community.

Jewels: riches; abundance.

Moon and Stars: universal influence.

Sun: radiant; generous; life-giving.

Upright Message: You are in a powerful position to help people right now. You may have become more comfortable and affluent in life and now want to contribute in a meaningful way. Your generosity will be much appreciated and will help the wider community. However small the gesture is, it will be put to good use and will really make someone's day. The more affluent you feel the grander your gestures are likely to be. If you are giving from the heart with no expectations, then you will be rewarded in so many ways for your kindness.

Reversed Message: In reversed position, be reminded to give from a selfless and heart-centered place. It feels good to give to those less fortunate, just be sure it isn't for the accolades or recognition. The flow of wealth outwards and back to you only really works if everyone in the equation feels equal and respected. Consider any biases or social judgments you may have. Just like the magpie is a misunderstood bird, are you supporting poverty without truly understanding it? Be careful that good intentions don't end up just a topic of discussion during your morning coffee or become another way to flaunt your wealth.

Seven of Pentacles (Flora's Garden)

Keywords: nurturing; sustainability; patience; reward.
Crystal: Mangano Calcite: calm; tranquility; patience; heart centered.

A woman relaxes in a beautiful garden savoring her well-deserved rest. The garden is mature and the vines grow high all around her. She sits in a space she has cleared beside an ornamental pillar, signifying a sense of achievement. Two bullfinches fly into view and a gray cat sits at her side, happy to be fussed over.

This scene of contentment has taken considerable effort but has been well worth it. The bullfinches symbolize patience and perseverance; they go about their business with dignity and an air of grace.

On her wrist the woman wears a small angel wing indicating her faith and her humble approach to work. Surrounding the scene are seven pentacles decorated with blossoms to show beauty, abundance and reward. The Seven of Pentacles' message is about patience and nurturing, allowing something to evolve after putting in the hard work needed.

Symbolic Healing and Guidance

Element: earth.

Qualities: security; stability; wealth; investment; the material realm.

Sevens: obstacles; challenges.

Bullfinches: patience; perseverance; dignity.

Pillar: strength; achievement.

Cat: contentment; calm; gentle; patience.

Angel Wing: blessed; humble; peace.

Upright Message: You are in no hurry to complete something because you know your reward is in the process and the enjoyment of a task. You appreciate the simple action of working on something for the pure pleasure derived. The tasks are not easy, but you will have such a sense of satisfaction from your efforts and gradual results. You will want to stop and admire things often, pause and drink in the beauty of everything you've created.

Reversed Message: There may be some frustration in thinking that you are working quite hard but only chipping away at the tasks. There may be lots of unexpected delays or perhaps your energy is depleted or pulled in too many different directions. It is time to regroup and reconsider your approach; try not to be too stubborn and single-minded with a task. Stop and use the time to make your life a little easier. The results will be worth it.

Eight of Pentacles (Jackalope Garden)

Keywords: nurturing; sustainability; patience; reward.
Crystal: Chrysoprase: self-improvement; enterprise; happiness; diligence.

A lush garden bustles with life, and seven blue jays work steadily on their tasks. Blue jays are industrious; they symbolize clarity, intellect and determination. Each of the birds represents a skill that the woman is perfecting right now; she may be a scholar or an apprentice, honing a craft or gaining further expertise. The jays carry with them seven pentacle charms to show the gifts being uncovered.

In the foreground, a magical jackalope hands the woman an eighth pentacle charm to show her that yet another reward is being earned. The woman allows herself a moment to daydream before continuing with her apprenticeship.

Symbolic Healing and Guidance

Element: earth.

Qualities: security; stability; wealth; investment; the material realm.

Eights: strength; prosperity; infinite success.

Blue Jays: stable; industrious; intellect; determination; skills.

Jackalope: daydream; reward; goal.

Wand: magic; divine gifts; self-improvement.

Upright Message: You are committing to honing your skills further. The universe has handed you all the tools you require, and you are excited about the work ahead. You are taking yourself away from the hustle and bustle in order to polish, perfect and develop your expertise. This is an investment in your future and the potential to be the best you can be. This period is worth any sacrifices in time and finance. Your efforts in the future will be rewarded.

Reversed Message: Be careful of slipping into the need for perfection. This is different than the pursuit of perfection, which is a moving, growing process. It may never be complete but every step, every mistake and every fine adjustment will bring you unlimited lessons and rewards. All successful people are standing on the rungs of the ladder, not sitting at the top with nothing more to do.

Nine of Pentacles (Scáthach)

Keywords: luxury; abundance; wealth; stability; nobility; status.
Crystal: Scottish Green Stone: guardian; nature; gifts; ancestry.

A noble woman sits surveying her land in the stillness of the night. Content and secure, she has built a stronghold with thistles protecting the boundaries. The great gardens are blossoming and reveal eight pentacle charms. A ninth flowering pentacle charm is worn by her cat companion.

Mature trees reach for the sky where a spectral owl flies into view, showing a level of completion and wisdom. This woman has been fortunate, and although she experienced ups and downs, she can now enjoy the fruits of her labor. At this point, she no longer needs to work too hard to retain this level of comfort. There is a quiet appreciation and gratitude for what she has achieved.

Symbolic Healing and Guidance

Element: earth.

Qualities: security; stability; wealth; investment; the material realm.

Nines: inner strength; life lessons; enlightenment.

Owl: wisdom.

Cat: comfort.

Castle (stronghold): security; status; wealth; protection.

Thistles/Blooms: protection; boundaries; growth.

Upright Message: The Nine of Pentacles encourages you to relax and enjoy your achievements. You have attained a level of comfort and maturity befitting a person of your status. There may be opportunities to really luxuriate in that contentedness with a well-deserved holiday, major renovation or a new home. Big dreams are within reach and possible in the material world at present. Enjoy these special moments.

Reversed Message: It is a wonderful time to enjoy your achievements. You may be worrying about whether or not you are worthy or deserving. Examine where these thoughts are coming from. If you look closely, you should know you worked hard and acted selflessly along the way. Sometimes, when you achieve this elevated status in life, others cannot wait to push you back down. Be aware of outside influences, jealous eyes, unkind thoughts and speculations directed at you. Be dignified and noble but ensure your protection surrounds you in the case of psychic attack, idle gossip and defamation. Know that any such opposition is built on untruths, so remember to enjoy your riches without fear.

Ten of Pentacles (The Family)

Keywords: security; family; support; comfort; wealth.
Crystal: Aragonite: solidify; earth; grounding; complete; settled.

A family is taking a stroll in a beautiful walled garden with their pet hounds. Ten pentacle charms encircle the portal in the wall, which looks upon a group of standing stones in the moonlight. The stones represent ancestors, lineage and family roots. The mature couple are secure in their home and surroundings; they are spiritually evolved and comfortable with their faith and divine connections. Their visiting daughter enjoys the comfort and security offered there. Two loyal hounds walk with them as treasured companions. Climbing blooms give way to butterflies and night gives over to day. The Ten of Pentacles card shows comfort, positivity and togetherness.

Symbolic Healing and Guidance

Element: earth.

Qualities: security; stability; wealth; investment; the material realm.

Tens: completion; accomplishment; content.

Dogs: loyalty; companionship; love.

Standing Stones: ancestors; heritage.

Blossoms and Butterflies: transformation; growth.

Family: security; bonds; safety.

Upright Message: The Ten of Pentacles represents successful fulfillment on the earthly, material plane. Some of the conventional ideas about security are portrayed in this card: gifts of heritage and lineage, successful career and good life choices, investment in your future, and solid family life, perhaps including a life-long partner and children of your own. While not all of these things are necessary to live out the Ten of Pentacles ideal, the card refers to the kind of security that comes from a comfortable, well-balanced life. Sometimes, this card appears when family support or gifts are being exchanged. Heirlooms, heritage and inheritance may also be indicated.

Reversed Message: The reversed position may indicate that you have everything you require for a good life, but it feels like it has made you complacent or too comfortable. Perhaps you need new activities to challenge you or you need to expand your horizons beyond this very material existence, which is becoming a bit superficial. It is a call to get out of your comfort zone. Or, perhaps someone in your family, maybe the teenage girl in this card, should be doing this if they are feeling a bit suffocated. It's all good; there is a safety net for you and your family to try new things.

Page of Pentacles (Huginn and Muninn)

Keywords: manifestation; messages; opportunities; aide.
Crystal: Black Onyx: balance; grounding;
material gain; manifestation.

This page stands in a rich, abundant poppy field, signifying they are dreaming big. In folkloric tradition, poppies are associated with sleep and dreams, but also abundance and riches. The ancients understood using poppies as a good crop rotation to invest in the soil and increase wheat yield.

This page may be entering an apprenticeship position, which will increase their financial security or career path. In such a powerful position of potential they can ask advice from the gods or divine realms. Odin's ravens Huginn and Muninn (thought and memory) sweep into view carrying messages and counsel. As well as prophesizing insight and investment in the future, the ravens are symbols of intelligence, adaptability and problem solving. They carry with them a pentacle charm as a sign of good fortune ahead.

Symbolic Healing and Guidance

Element: earth.

Qualities: security; stability; wealth; investment; the material realm.

Pages: apprentice; potential; creative energy.

Poppies: dreams; aspirations; luxury; riches; manifestation.

Ravens: intellect; prophecy; investment; adaptable.

Upright Message: The Page of Pentacles is looking to turn their dreams into a reality. They are focused in the earthly, material realm and have goals to furnish it with riches and comfort. This card may represent the beginning of a new career path or training position that will help yield such rewards. You are likely adept at using "thoughts and memory" in this position and the path you are choosing is likely to be very lucrative. The Page of Pentacles also brings in an invested energy, things like speculation, statistics, shares and investment loans may play a role in your next steps.

Reversed Message: The reversed position probably means you just have a little more research to do before you dive in. The Page of Pentacles is ruled by earth so is not a big risk taker. Take the time to project that career path, read the small print, study the stock market; whatever it takes to plan with more confidence. Be careful, however, of getting stuck in the daydream stage as some of the opportunities may be time sensitive and may not be available forever. Shine a light on any shadows holding you back like disadvantages from childhood or experiences of poverty. You may be the first in your family to attend university or have ambitions above your social class. This card brings reassurance that you can do this; just examine any baggage that you need to clear and let go of.

Knight of Pentacles (Contemplation)

Keywords: contemplation; routine; conservative; assessment; planning.
Crystal: Lavender Quartz: calm; measured; joyful; unconditional love; contentment.

This knight stands ready in a contemplative pose holding out a pentacle coin. A spirit horse hovers at their shoulder, indicating actions not yet manifest. The Knight of Pentacles is perhaps the most laid back and gentle of the knights. They are very happy to hang back and contemplate the possibilities before them. A ploughed field is seen in the landscape showing ready potential and the willingness to take the next step and put in the work required. A windmill gently turns with a steady clack, marking the passing of time in an unhurried way. The knight stands in a beautiful field of wildflowers, knowing that steadiness and patience will pay off. On her armor are more blooms and yellow roses, which symbolize joy and contentment.

Around her neck is a spider amulet, a powerful creation symbol representing patience, endurance, repetition, the cycles of nature and powerful manifestation.

Symbolic Healing and Guidance

Element: earth.

Qualities: security; stability; wealth; investment; the material realm

Knights: action; vitality; service; honor.

Horse: spirit; divine gifts; wisdom; power; freedom.

Spider: patience; endurance; planning; creation.

Yellow Roses: simple joy; contentment.

Field: potential; steady work; repetition.

Windmill: gentle; time; patience; steady movement; repetition.

Upright Message: You are drawn to planning and preparing for your tasks ahead. You know there will be lots of work coming up and will want to contemplate the best methods and resources.

You are attracted to routine, especially right now. Tasks that are repetitive bring you joy and a sense of satisfaction; you find solace in the simple meditation of routine activities and chores. These offer time to contemplate and dream for the future.

Reversed Message: This card is a call and a reminder to develop a plan and a strategy for your goals. They require this input and won't simply manifest of their own accord. Lay the foundations, do the groundwork and be prepared for some patient nurturing and repetitive work at this stage.

Conversely, you may be feeling a little stuck in the routine and mundane aspects of a situation. Perhaps the joy has gone from this simple lifestyle, and you need to look at next steps. Take a leaf from this knight's book and get excited about a new plan. No need to dive in quickly; just start to explore the possibilities and you will get moving again.

Queen of Pentacles (Queen of Charms)

Keywords: practical; generous; protective; security.
Crystal: Topaz: confidence; generosity; nurturing; sovereign; self-worth.

This queen invites you into her realm and holds out a gift of a pentacle charm. This ruler is kind and generous; she protects her subjects and is likely to be a maternal figure. Her throne is surrounded by flowers and foliage showing abundance and her alignment with nature. The exotic bird perched beside her shows her love of beauty, communication and transformation. The goat companion by her side indicates a love and enjoyment of the sensual pleasures in life. This queen has much in common with the Empress, but here she is more of the vehicle and less of the vessel, playing a very active role in her realm. Her love of opulence and the things that money can buy is echoed in her sumptuous clothing and elaborate crown. Around her neck she wears jewels and amulets, including a rabbit for good fortune and fertility.

Symbolic Healing and Guidance

Element: earth.

Qualities: security; stability; wealth; investment; the material realm.

Queens: feminine; mature; nurturing; ruler.

Bird: beauty; communication; transformation.

Rabbit: good fortune; fertility.

Goat: enjoyment; wealth; sensuality; pleasure.

Butterflies: transformation.

Upright Message: This queen is a real powerhouse, managing the material realm and her finances meticulously, while providing care and nurturing to those in her charge. Think of a powerful businesswoman who is also a mother, juggling various roles while fitting in time to enjoy herself and her hard-earned rewards.

You may be in this position, where you are independent and equipped to handle anything on your own. This has afforded you success and good fortune. There is still a warmness about you, and you would do anything to help those who need it. Ultimately, you have remained grounded, and people really appreciate your practical resourcefulness and ability to have a good time. This queen may well have a romantic partner, but she earns more or has a higher status than her mate. She could be the main or sole breadwinner; but this doesn't matter to her; other attributes impress her more.

Reversed Message: In this position, you might be feeling stressed or out of alignment. Too many things might be competing for your attention. You need to strike a balance between work and home life, friends and family, or other similar social conflicts. Examine what is truly important to you and eliminate any commitments that really don't interest you. Learn to say "No" to the more superficial things in life.

King of Pentacles (King of Charms)

Keywords: wealth; prosperity; leadership; strength.
Crystal: Cinnabar: strength; vitality; virility; stable.

The King of Pentacles dominates a large and comfortable throne, which is embellished with bull horns. His cloaks are embroidered with rich, fertile leaves and seeds, and on his robes are more Taurean imagery. This king sits in a lush landscape and in the distance you can see his large, comfortable residence. Yet, he doesn't require much pomp and fanfare; he prefers the more earthly enjoyments of the world.

The king holds a large pentacle coin showing his stability and wealth. Around his neck are various amulets showing his achievements and his path: a spiral for eternity and links to the divine, a bell for meditation and mindfulness, a pendulum for counsel and prediction, and a labyrinth for his ability to navigate obstacles. This king has confronted many things and conquered all challenges to achieve a very comfortable position. He is a loyal and giving king.

Symbolic Healing and Guidance

Element: earth.

Qualities: security; stability; wealth; investment; the material realm.

Kings: masculine; mature; generous; ruler.

Bulls: virility; strength; vitality; Taurean energy.

Labyrinth: challenges; journey.

Upright Message: This king is reliable, faithful and generous. He is that solid presence who can be depended on to look after his charges well. The King of Pentacles is likely to have strong fatherly energies; he likes to nurture and provide for. He may be gregarious and enjoys a party or two, certainly rich food and wine will appear in his world. People enjoy being around this king and feel reassured and safe with him.

You may find yourself in a position to mentor or to help a young person reach their potential. You are aligned with nature and its resources, which indicate the calling to help with animals or environmental issues. Self-sufficiency and the fruits of the land interest you;

perhaps tending to a vineyard for your own enjoyment or getting involved in a community garden and giving back.

Reversed Message: In the reversed position, this king can lean toward excess and stubbornness, if you think of the shadow aspects of Taurus. Watch out for over-indulgence, over-spending or a tendency not to listen and bulldoze over other people's ideas. It may be time to curb spending or consumption and become more relaxed about your controlling aspects. At his root, this king is kind and generous without being domineering.

Suit of Swords

Ace of Swords (The Navigator)

Keywords: divine gifts; intellect; ideas; innovator; navigator.
Crystal: Icelandic Spar: navigation; clarity; focus; direction; new journey.

The navigator holds his sword steady in front of him. The moon looms large in the background and clouds roll in, showing this to be a gift from the divine; perhaps a new idea, a revelation or a fledgling plan to stimulate the intellect into action. The hilt of the sword is shaped like a crown, showing that there will be success; however, the blade is wrapped in ribbons and leaves, indicating that the idea is not ready for implementation. This card is full of possibilities. This ace is a navigator and an architect of plans who uses his cerebral energy to move things ahead. Around his neck he carries a compass to draw up plans and in his pouch a piece of Icelandic spar, which will be used to navigate. Thistles spring up to protect his wonderful new ideas and innovations. The ice peaks rise in the background showing the exciting highs and lows of the journey ahead. It isn't an entirely new path, but he will make his own mark along the way and carve out a unique approach.

His clothes are richly embroidered with images of helpful animals: a hawk (air and overview), snake (transformation), ibis (intellect and communication), squirrel (preparation, strategy), and by his side is a wolf both loyal and free.

Symbolic Healing and Guidance

Element: air.

Qualities: truth; intellect; justice.

Aces: pure potential; beginnings; optimism; divine gifts; passion.

Wolf: loyalty; freedom.

Crown: success.

Ribbons, Bells and Leaves: fledgling ideas.

Compass: intellect; architect; planning.

Hawk: air; divine gifts; foresight.

Snake: transformation; beginnings.

Ibis: intellect; communication; planning.

Squirrel: preparation; strategy.

Upright Message: It is a favorable time to start new projects and make new plans; ideas and inspirations are flowing. This Ace asks you to plan and develop, to seek truth and more knowledge. A clear and measured approach will bring success.

Reversed Message: You may be on the cusp of a wonderful new idea or project. You need to work out some details, but in the meantime, you should protect or document your idea. There will be a short delay or time of planning and cultivating before you are ready to reveal more.

Two of Swords (Trust)

Keywords: decisions; options; balance; contemplation.
Crystal: Banded Agate: grounding; balance; yin and yang energies.

A woman wearing a blindfold kneels in a barren desert landscape of fine sand. Suspended in a delicate balance are two large swords. Several piles of pebbles are stacked nearby and appear to be steady despite the shifting nature of the sand. This card is about decisions, choices and weighing up the right path to take next. The woman's head is bowed in deep thought. A wind blows clouds across the moon and stirs the sand in the scene, but the woman remains still and grounded in her contemplation. She knows she must go deep within to find the answers to her dilemma.

The Two of Swords expects a certain amount of trust that this pause is the right course of action for now. The woman holds a compass to represent her inner searching for direction. And a small owl flies overhead holding a pendulum to help with divination and intuition. A period of introspection is indicated.

Symbolic Healing and Guidance

Element: air.

Qualities: truth; intellect; justice.

Twos: balance; comfort; self-control; duality; yin yang; stop and go; decisions; choices.

Owl: wisdom; introspection.

Compass: decisions; direction; intuition.

Pendulum: divination; advice; self-counsel.

Stones: grounding; steady; pause.

Upright Message: The Two of Swords indicates a big decision to make where the outcomes are hidden or unpredictable. The only course of action is to pause and use all the resources at hand. A pause for further contemplation will allow you to slow down and stay grounded. You might need to get down and be physically close to the earth. A period of introspection may give you the best options that consider both thought (head) and emotion (heart). Using this approach, you can trust that your decision will be the best at this time, although all outcomes should be quite favorable.

Reversed Message: You may feel stuck in this decision that you have to make. It appears outcomes might not be all that favorable whatever you decide. If your meditation doesn't bring clarity, then you might benefit from taking off your blindfold and relying on your physical senses to guide you. You may also need to trust the further expertise of others to help. Examine all your options in this vein and listen intently.

Three of Swords (Deirdre of the Sorrows)

Keywords: hurt; pain; grief; sorrow; release; trauma; healing.
Crystal: Apophyllite: deep healing; heart center; trauma release; grief.

A woman sits in the cold snow. Her heart is pierced by three swords representing a great loss and feelings of grief and sorrow. In the snow three drops of blood are being watched over by a crow who is symbolic of great change. In this card, the change is difficult as there needs to be a release of pain and trauma. The piercing of the heart is the first step in this release and healing. Although tears stream down the woman's face, this also triggers her to turn and look determinedly to the future. She is suffering but she is not broken.

On the tree there are some poisonous fungi, which is a reminder not to transmute hurt into anger and revenge. Go through the emotions but don't allow them to linger and fester. Swords are representative of air and movement, so be assured this too shall pass.

Symbolic Healing and Guidance

Element: air.

Qualities: truth; intellect; justice.

Threes: balance; solidity; support;
divine blessings; consolidation.

Crow: change; death; rebirth.

Blood: pain and loss.

Tears: grief; release.

Upright Message: Sometimes this card can indicate a broken heart from an unexpected break up or loss. Some of life's major hurts can catch you unexpectedly and throw you into a tailspin. It could also mean that someone has hurt you deeply with their words or actions. You could be attracting that sort of energy and may be feeling exceptionally sensitive to careless words. In any case, it is something that has brought out the rawest of emotions, perhaps triggering old wounds and trauma. The card is a call to examine this hurt, to feel deeply then release. There is every indication you will come back stronger, even if it doesn't feel that way right now.

Reversed Message: When reversed, this can be a sign of psychological or physical self-harm. That inner voice could be dialed up high, constantly directing hateful thoughts toward yourself. It could be that you are ruminating on the words of others and directing them in on yourself, spinning stories wider and bigger for the maximum hurt. It may be time to address the old wounds and traumas that keep resurfacing and keep you locked in this place. People will certainly mirror them back at you until you work through them. Similarly, someone or some situation may have caused these feelings, either intentionally or not. You will need time to process, grieve and protect yourself while going through this. This may be a longer period to get through, but you will prevail.

Four of Swords (Pause)

Keywords: rest; recuperate; recover; meditate; recalibrate.
Crystal: Unakite: heart-centered healing; gentle; recovery; forgiveness; balance; surrender.

A woman sits in the lotus position with four swords balanced around her. Her eyes are closed and she is suspended in a period of meditation and rest. This pause is self-imposed as she knows she must surrender to complete rest and retreat after a difficult period. This four brings back balance, equilibrium and recuperation.

A bat is tucked under her robes and moths appear around her, indicating the darker aspects of herself that need to be healed in the shadows or subconscious dream states. The bat can also represent transformation and letting go. Bat energy will help address feelings of stress, anxiety and overwhelm. Similarly, the moths are a powerful emblem of regeneration and rejuvenation. The woman wears a moth with spread wings on her hat to show that healing is quietly taking place.

This period of seclusion and recovery is essential to gather your resources for the next stage of your journey.

Symbolic Healing and Guidance

Element: air.

Qualities: truth; intellect; justice.

Fours: robust; solid; strong; complete; stable.

Bat: transformation; shadow work; health; vitality.

Moths: healing; transmutation; regeneration.

Upright Message: A period of recovery is required after a troubling time. You may be handling feelings of stress, anxiety and general overwhelm. This card calls for you to pause and enter a period of seclusion and recuperation. The most important thing is to settle your mind, regulate your breath and allow the body's remarkable ability to heal naturally. Be kind to yourself; don't push for any activity or contact but do explore mindful techniques and meditation if you feel called to it. The woman here is protected on all sides by the swords that surround her, so she feels safe to go ahead with this much needed pause. Her message is to relax and look after your self-care.

Reversed Message: You may have burnt yourself out emotionally and physically. The reversed message is a strict one to take this period of self-care very seriously. If you can, get away to a secluded retreat or spa but certainly take an extended period off work. Ask for support if needed but be very clear about boundaries. Switch off devices and ignore social media, the news and television for this period. The healing work needs complete silence and rest. It may take some time and discipline to detach from work or relationships but you will feel brand new and ready for the world again before long.

Five of Swords (The Vanquished)

Keywords: standoff; stalemate; conflict; disagreements; competition; battle of wills.
Crystal: Rhodonite: forgiveness; letting go; acceptance; moving on; empathy

A young woman clutches three swords as she turns her back on the scene. There is a feather in her cap and a feeling of victory, but there is no satisfaction in this outcome. In her heart the feelings of hate or the need to conquer have dissipated and are no longer threatening at all. Left behind on the ground are two more abandoned swords. The defeated, the perceived enemy, has shapeshifted into a hare that is making a hasty retreat. Did the woman really win or was this just a case of two losses? The conflict takes place outside the church yard walls, indicating that this confrontation was not endorsed by the divine nature of the sparring duo. The young warrior walks off through a tangle of high weeds and wildflowers showing the complexity of the situation, which could so easily be cut back and cleared up. At the moment, a stalemate looks to be the outcome.

Symbolic Healing and Guidance

Element: air.

Qualities: truth; intellect; justice.

Fives: conflict; discord; miscommunication.

Church: holy; divine; higher self.

Hare: shift; shapeshifter; confusion.

Upright Message: A tussle for power is indicated in some way. You may have recently won an argument or had a promotion or recognition that somehow doesn't feel deserved. Perhaps you were overly competitive or even aggressive. Maybe you cheated or manipulated events? In any case it feels like you won at a cost and may have lost ground in other ways you have not yet considered. A stalemate has been reached and you could try to make amends or apologize if you think your victory was at the expense of others. It's not too late to do that or accept that differing opinions remain unresolved.

Reversed Message: A conflict of some sort has been going round and round to no avail. Each party is not listening to the other and the belief systems are too ingrained for either to admit defeat. It is time to make peace and amends; it is all you can do to resolve things. It may feel nice to get the upper hand and feel like you are winning, but before long the opposition will come back for more, thinking they are in the right. To resume a peaceful life without resentment and anger you will need to let go, forgive and move on.

Six of Swords (Departure)

Keywords: departing; rites of passage; letting go; moving on.
Crystal: Tree Agate: good luck; strength; new growth; putting down roots.

A boat leaves the harbor heading for new shores. Aboard is a woman traveling light; she is leaving everything behind for a new chapter. Her hair is silver from a life well lived and she is at the stage where she has no responsibilities or cares tying her down. Sharing her voyage of discovery are her beloved pets of the canine and feline variety. She accepts both just as they are; these are her companions and partners for the next part of her journey.

At this stage in life, she is independent, creative and resourceful, wearing warm clothes all hand embroidered, knitted and woven. On the bough of her boat a little carved mask sticks out its tongue playfully at a bemused fish below. Four swords protect the launch and take off; two more sit in the boat just in case they are needed later. In the distant shore there are signs of a small community waiting to welcome the traveler. There is a feeling of freedom and anticipation.

Symbolic Healing and Guidance

Element: air.

Qualities: truth; intellect; justice.

Sixes: abundance; balance; stability.

Church: community.

Boat: departing; letting go; freedom; independence, travel.

Cat and Dog: loyalty; companionship.

Crone: a rite of passage; wisdom; independence; resourceful.

Upright Message: You are moving into a new chapter. Life may not have been easy lately and the waters around you are still choppy, but looking ahead everything indicates clear sailing. There is a sense of letting go of unnecessary baggage and just taking what you need with you. It is time to be confident about the gifts you have accumulated and what you have to offer in new situations. This is enough to get you started and the rest will unfold in time. Keep your humor and creative spirit alive.

Reversed Message: It could be that you are resisting change or doubting this pending journey. There may be sadness for things left behind or your old life. There needs to be recognition that this is an important rite of passage for you. Once you accept that things are changing in a big way, it will feel easier and more supportive. This transition may be quite profound and spiritual. It is a huge opportunity for growth if you avoid the inevitable struggles as you adjust.

Seven of Swords (The Opportunist)

Keywords: departing; betrayal; double cross; strategy; self-preservation.
Crystal: Black Tourmaline Quartz: protection; strong boundaries; self-preservation.

A woman steals away from the camp under the cover of darkness. In her backpack she carries five swords, while two more have been left in the camp. She needs to get away on her own terms, so she is relying on some trickery and stealth. It is not an easy decision; she is leaving behind a lush oasis and the support of the community for the barren landscape of the desert.

The departure may be temporary until all the issues surrounding this decision can be worked out. She has left two swords behind to suggest she may return, and the theft of the other swords may feel necessary for her self-preservation. In her mind, she may perceive this as borrowing with no real ill intent. Something in this apparently idyllic setup makes her uneasy and her decision is swift and executed in secret.

In her arms is a small monkey companion who chooses to travel with her out of curiosity and free will; he represents quick-wittedness, strategy and survival.

Symbolic Healing and Guidance

Element: air.

Qualities: truth; intellect; justice.

Sevens: obstacles; challenges.

Camp: community; resources; danger; secrets.

Monkey: strategy; dexterity; intellect; trickery.

Moon: secrets; hidden; betrayal.

Upright Message: There is a situation you desire to keep secret. This may involve pulling the wool over someone's eyes, trickery and deception. In your mind, these things might be necessary to get through something challenging. This is probably just your pride or ego speaking; you should examine the clandestine behavior and determine if it is really worth it. At some point, you will be caught or called out on these actions. Your intent may be self-preservation and to do no harm, but in this situation, someone is going to feel hurt or betrayed.

Reversed Message: The reversed position is an indicator of inner deceit. You may be lying to yourself about your actions and motivations, or you don't want to face up to your behaviors. If a pattern is forming, it can become ingrained and more difficult to overcome later. The key in this case is to uncover the shadow tendencies, face your impostor syndrome, denial and dark secrets. If left unattended they can fester and lead to stress and shame. It is best to get help now, to confront these hidden traits and build bridges where necessary. Work on the end results of integrity, authenticity and healing.

Eight of Swords (The Martyr)

Keywords: restriction; bondage; self-sacrifice; victim mentality; martyrdom.
Crystal: Shungite: purification; release; absorption.

A woman is bound and blindfolded in the center of eight swords. On first appearance she seems captive and sacrificial. On closer inspection it becomes evident that her bindings are quite minimal and if she removed her blindfold, she would see the scissors hanging around her neck. Freedom is really just a snip away and these restrictions are of her own making. A group of sparrows look on in bemusement at her predicament. They are wondering whether to start a chorus to jolt her awareness, even the one flying past seems to make no impact. Sparrows represent empowerment, allies, community and safety, all of the things that she perceives to be inaccessible. The symbols of each planet embellish the hilts of each blade. They reveal that help is at hand from the universe and it is always available to us. On the blindfold is a representation of the all-seeing eye, which indicates a deeper intuition within. If she watches the self-sabotaging thoughts go by, she might reach that place of understanding and internal release.

Symbolic Healing and Guidance

Element: air.

Qualities: truth; intellect; justice.

Eights: strength; prosperity;
infinite success.

Planets: universal support.

Sparrows: empowerment;
community; protection.

Blue Moon: growth; self-discovery;
depth of wisdom.

Upright Message: There is a feeling of being trapped and immobilized. Right now, you can't see a way forward and don't recognize the options that may be open to you. There are limiting thoughts at play, low vibration ruminations and unnecessary worry. The Eight of Swords asks you to go deep within yourself to separate your current mindset from actual reality. Learn to recognize the self-sabotage and victim mentality that only keeps you stuck. Surrender and trust that you are supported, then take off the blinder and take one step at a time. Breakthroughs are close and there are major lessons to learn with this eight.

Reversed Message: It could be that limiting patterns and self-sabotaging behaviors have become deeply ingrained and are causing you anxiety. You trust yourself so little that you are frozen and afraid to move forward. Unfortunately, you trust others even less and may be blaming them for your pain or your predicament. Something has to change, and the reversed position can indicate a breakthrough if you are prepared to work on releasing the deeper issues at play.

Nine of Swords (The Night Terror)

Keywords: fears; nightmares; insomnia; anxiety.
Crystal: Chevron Amethyst: calming; clearing energy; aura repair; restorative sleep; dream recall.

A girl sits up in bed, covering her face with both hands. Nine blades surround her; eight are floating through the night, suspended in the clouds, revealing this to be a dreamscape world.

A gargoyle-like demon looming over her represents the night terror that threatens her sleep. Painted on her hands are markings to ward off the "evil eye" and one of the blades sits beside her on the bed as protection.

A little cat is tucked in beside her, but also doesn't want to acknowledge the demons in the night. The message of this card asks us to go deep and confront the very roots of our fears and anxiety. These are often deeply anchored in childhood conditioning or submerged memories.

The root causes of depression, anxiety, insomnia and stress are usually the same regardless of the situation, event or immediate trigger. Understanding the story and the root cause will help you deal with these debilitating conditions and your feelings of distress.

Symbolic Healing and Guidance

Element: air.

Qualities: truth; intellect; justice.

Nines: inner strength; big lessons; enlightenment.

Clouds: dreams.

Demon: night terror; hidden fears; anxiety.

Upright Message: There is a great deal of stress and worry in your life at the moment. Dark ruminations, negative thoughts and catastrophizing are present during the day and are keeping you up at night. The sense of overwhelm is so bad that it is manifesting in physical ways. You are still able to do a lot to help yourself, but before you can address self-care you need to get to the root of the psychological conditioning behind your fears. Examine your thoughts of scarcity, loss or abandonment as possible driving factors. Then, you can begin to work through solutions to these challenges. Introducing a good nighttime care ritual can bring calm during this very important healing time.

Reversed Message: The good news is you may be close to seeing some light at the end of this dark tunnel. Nines are close to completing that cycle and all things that come to pass. However, you may be so affected that you are unable to see this hope. Self-help rituals are advocated but you may need extra help to calm things down before you can do that work. Meditation, therapy, acupuncture or hypnosis from a qualified professional can bring comfort and relief. Line up all your resources and coping mechanisms to get through this phase.

Ten of Swords (The Defeated)

Keywords: defeat; the end; release; end of suffering.
Crystal: Golden Healer: deep healing; access to high vibration; crown chakra activation.

A man lies face down on the ground with ten needle-like blades embedded into his back and neck, showing his pain and suffering. He is pinned down and defeated. He has given up on life; his energy and life-force appear to be leaving him. But the blades are beautiful and bejeweled, showing that there is some value in this very oppressive situation

A small crystal amulet is wrapped around his arm, offering some healing and comfort, which he clings to. He must surrender completely and accept this process. The Ten of Swords is a metaphoric death and rebirth card. It can indicate painful endings but if you look again, the man is surrounded by new foliage as he lays there unaware of what is ahead of him. It is also a card of ultimate release. The grass around him is beginning to grow again and the wisdom of his ancestors is represented by an ancient stone circle.

In the distance, a beautiful vista of bustling new life speaks of community, support and hope. A castle sits on the hill, showing the riches to be discovered. A bridge leads to a cheerful little village with welcoming hearths sending smoke up into the sky. A wide river flows toward the distressed figure and a boat is moored there to transport the man to a better place. A small chapel sits on high ground, showing a return of faith in whatever form that may be.

Symbolic Healing and Guidance

Element: air.

Qualities: truth; intellect; justice.

Tens: completion; accomplishment; content.

Chapel: faith; hope; spiritual support.

Blades: suffering; endings; value; lessons.

Castle: recovery; health; wealth.

River: lifeline.

Village: community; support.

Standing Stones: ancestors; guides; reassurance; wisdom.

Upright Message: As a metaphor for death and new beginnings this card signifies a completion of a cycle, as with all tens. This ending however, is painful and abrupt and may bring a sense of loss and suffering. It could be a painful end to a relationship, a bereavement or dismissal. Whatever the situation, it will feel like complete devastation and will render you defeated and frail. Yet this card is a message to heal and release and be hopeful in even the smallest measure right now. This too shall pass.

Reversed Message: You are clinging to your suffering and defeat so tightly right now. Refusing to meet it and transmute it, you remain caught in a cycle of grief and despair. This will only prolong the situation until you can see a chink of light in the darkness. The first stage is to surrender and accept. Then, seize with all your might any glimmer of hope emerging.

Page of Swords (The Apprentice)

Keywords: new ideas; curiosity; communication; apprentice.
Crystal: Blue Calcite: self expression; communication; creative thinking.

A lone figure stands inside a stone circle with her sword raised in ceremony. The tip of her blade stirs the leaves of an overhanging tree. New ideas are forming, exciting new approaches to uncover and discover. This page is tapping into the ancient energy and wisdom that runs through the land, but she is ready to transmute it into action and doing, in line with her affinity to the element air.

Two crows enter the scene and more take to the skies. Crows have powerful insight and intellect, they can also indicate change and transformation. A number of crows show a great number of possibilities and directions to go in.

This page is richly dressed and adorned with amulets and bells. They may be in a privileged position of apprenticeship and study. There is potential to rise and lead in areas of communication.

Enjoy the high energy and many inspirations that present themselves at this time.

Symbolic Healing and Guidance

Element: air.

Qualities: truth; intellect; justice.

Pages: apprentice; potential; creativity energy.

Standing Stones: earth energy; ancestors; guides; wisdom.

Tree: ideas; inspirations.

Crows: insight; intellect; possibilities; change; transformation.

Moon: mystery.

Upright Message: The Page of Swords card is a call to try new things and trust the process. You will learn by doing; you may not get it all right, but the process and initiation will be very valuable. You may be in a position that allows you to experiment and try out new ideas. You might be exploring new beliefs and doctrines or simply keeping your options open. Use this time of learning wisely and enjoy it. Gifts from the universe will reward your curiosity and spontaneity.

Reversed Message: Stay open to ideas and opinions from others right now. You are on your own path of discovery and learning, and may be very enthusiastic about new ideas. Try to stay flexible and open to valuable insights from others, regardless of your perceptions or judgments. Also, be careful of flitting too quickly from one project to the next. Take your time and do your research. The "devil is in the details" so stay a while and deepen your understanding.

Knight of Swords (The Challenge)

Keywords: action; ambition; success.
Crystal: Dumortierite: bolsters confidence; strength; encourages fearlessness; overcoming phobias.

This knight is poised for action. He is driven, focused and highly successful. His mount is a powerful black panther, a high vibrational being of sharp intelligence and devastating beauty. His helmet sports wings, showing his swift nature, ready to charge ahead and get things done. He is wearing a crystal on the front of his helmet for clarity and vision. The knight's blade is short, not long, showing his quick nature and intimate process; he is prepared for close combat. He is a focused yet hasty worker, sometimes impatient but full of vitality and adventure, with a killer instinct. The lush foliage surrounding the duo point to abundance, achievement and success, indicating that the knight's charge-ahead, positive attitude will prevail.

Symbolic Healing and Guidance

Element: air.

Qualities: truth; intellect; justice.

Knights: action; vitality; service; honor.

Crystal: focus; clarity; vision.

Panther: power; protection;
courage; intellect.

Upright Message: It is time to be assertive and push ahead with your goals. A positive "can do" attitude will get you everywhere right now. Take the exam, ask for the promotion, start the new project; your efforts will be noticed and rewarded by the people that matter. You may be too busy getting things done to realize this but someone important has been captivated by your inner panther. Expect opportunities and success to come your way.

Reversed Message: This knight sometimes moves with haste. You may be feeling restless, on edge and a bit scattered. Watch out for multi-tasking, overloading and overwhelm. Being proactive is still the best thing, but slow down a bit and be more mindful of each stage. This knight has feline resources of focus and patience to balance him, so use those well but rein in your impatient nature for the best results. Think of a cat that needs to sleep much of the day to optimize its active hours.

Queen of Swords (The Diamond Queen)

Keywords: fair; judgment; progressive; equality; direct.
Crystal: Diamond: strength; invincible; integrity.

Sitting proudly on her throne, this queen holds a sword of bronze and gold before her, to cast favor rather than to strike down. This ruler is fair and just; she emulates the Justice card and exercises great integrity. Seated nearby are two cats, relaxed, aloof, sovereign and assured in their position by her side.

The Queen of Swords is fiercely independent. She rules with strength and directness. In this deck, she is depicted future facing. Her communication skills are direct, and she likes to cut to the point and move forward. Her concern is for the greater good and the bigger picture. She can seem cold and distanced with strong boundaries, but her focus for her subjects is self-realization, freedom and justice. There is an underlying compassion that is more practical and solution based.

The butterflies on her headdress symbolize freedom and liberty. They are seen flying around her sword too, suggesting movement, progress and transformation. Metamorphosis is one of nature's most miraculous ways to reinvent itself and transmute into something beautiful. She is associated with the butterfly and, in particular, its lesson of transformation.

On her throne is the symbol of Fawohodie, the West African symbol of independence, freedom and emancipation. The throne is also cloaked with moons and stars to show her far-gazing universal interests. Hearts are woven into her braids to show her focus on love and compassion. Her adornments and surroundings are infused with gold. Her intent is always to give back, so everything she receives is magnified for noble causes. A coin purse sits at her feet for anyone who needs help.

Symbolic Healing and Guidance

Element: air.

Qualities: truth; intellect; justice.

Queens: feminine; mature; nurturing; ruler.

Cats: intent; self-assured; aloof; confident.

Butterflies: transformation; change; progress; the power to influence.

Blue Cloud: heart-centered decisions;
throat chakra; mutable.

Coin Purse: fairness; generosity.

Upright Message: Your gifts include quiet reservation, unbiased judgment and a cool rational approach. Although you might seem a little aloof you are devoted to humanitarian interests. Perhaps there is a legal matter or diplomatic mission to take care of. The Queen of Swords will bring self-assured energy and righteous compassion to proceedings.

Reversed Message: When reversed, the message is a reminder to balance the traits of this queen carefully. She is neither too emotional nor too stern and cold, as neither extreme serves her well. The lesson here is to not let your heart rule your head in difficult decisions. It is also a reminder to keep your power in check and not judge too harshly or act in a cruel, dismissive way.

King of Swords (The King of Reason)

Keywords: intellect; expect; authority; truth.
Crystal: Staurolite: truth; clarity; reason; intellect; science.

The King of Swords sits confidently on his throne facing forward; his gaze is direct and transparent. This king is concerned with intellectual thoughts, reasoning, truth and science. He exudes an air of quiet calm and holds his sword steady on his right shoulder, showing a nod to his intuitive side, for he is fair and balanced rather than rigid in his mindset.

High on the hill stands a tower of knowledge, a library filled with both academic knowledge and the arts. Gentle clouds drift to the valley below and settle near an ancient monument, highlighting knowledge from the past. His cat companion looks to the future to show his progressiveness and understanding of new ideas, science and solutions. This king is surrounded with foliage showing an abundance of growth and progress. The toadstools hint at the magic in this deck but also hidden truths and universal knowledge. The blooms and vines are echoed on his throne where a small butterfly symbolizes transformative energy.

Symbolic Healing and Guidance

Element: air.

Qualities: truth; intellect; justice.

Kings: masculine; mature; generous; ruler.

Butterfly: transformation.

Library: knowledge; science; academia; the arts.

Stone Monument: ancient wisdom.

Cat: progressive; focused; forward looking.

Upright Message: You may have gained a position of expertise or specialist knowledge in your life. The king indicates an opportunity to use it for good intent. People respect what you have to say and will listen right now. Work within the realms of academia will be well received and there may be green lights for further research or implementation in your given field. There will be situations where you are asked to give expert advice and counsel. You will be in a strong position to help something progress meaningfully.

Reversed Message: As with all positions of power and authority, this reversed perspective is to watch ego. Be sure not to undervalue the input of others just because you are the given authority on a subject. Intellectual superiority tends to dampen real progress, which calls for an open mind and the ability to reexamine the current ways of thinking. Remain open-minded and curious.

Suit of Wands

Ace of Wands (The Visionary)

Keywords: creativity; growth; potential; vision.
Crystal: Carnelian: courage; creativity; vitality; motivation; energizing.

The woman carries a single wand sprouting new leaves symbolizing potential, and the birthing of ideas and visions. Creativity is fertile and potent, and many ideas are rolling in on all sides with the clouds—gifts from the divine. The garden in the foreground is full of new blooms and thistles that protect these tentative beginnings as they gain momentum. The owl represents the wisdom and knowledge that comes with the night and its dream worlds. It carries the seeds of creativity and jewels of optimism being birthed from the darkness. The white cat appears alert and actively looking to the future and sunny days ahead.

The woman wears a spider amulet, which represents artistry and divine manifestation. The spider is one of the oldest creator beings we know and is thought to take divine potential and weave it into being. In the background, a beautiful castle rises up, showing the possibilities ahead and the ability to aim high and think big.

Symbolic Healing and Guidance

Element: fire.

Qualities: warm; energetic; charismatic; creative; purposeful; positive; ambitious.

Aces: pure potential; beginnings; optimism; divine gifts; passion.

Castle: ambition; success; aiming high.

Owl: night; wisdom; birth; dreams.

Cat: alert; purpose; momentum; potential.

Spider: creation; manifestation.

Upright Message: It is a favorable time to follow your passions and seek your calling. Ideas and ambitions are fertile and abundant. The Ace of Wands card points to exciting new beginnings and successful outcomes. You are in a great position to manifest your desires and plant the seeds of exciting new developments.

Reversed Message: In reverse, this card can show an abundance of ideas that lack purpose and direction. There may be too much going on and too many possibilities to choose from, which can overwhelm you quickly and cause you to lose energy or motivation. The best thing to do would be to ground yourself and get balanced and relaxed. Cultivate space around your amazing ideas and tend to them carefully, protecting their tender shoots. From this point, you will start to see the potential growing again with renewed interest.

Two of Wands (The Dreamer)

Keywords: progress; new horizons; planning; goals.
Crystal: Amethyst: decision making; clarity; planning; intuition; vision; third eye.

The woman looks out from her castle battlements holding a globe in her hand. A level of success and comfort has been achieved and now she sets her sights on more ambitious goals. Outside the castle walls there is a moat, which provides protection for what she has accomplished but also an impediment to further progress. In the distance, there are high hills to climb and explore; they represent the various challenges in this next stage. The hills give way to exotic new places to visit and enjoy. It is a time of careful planning. She holds a wand out purposefully, while keeping another within the castle walls. The card indicates decisions and exploration, while keeping all options open and maintaining a measure of safety and stability. Her loyal dog may serve as a trusty guide and fellow adventurer, reminding her of home comforts and the security she has built. The sirin perched on her wand sings beautiful songs of far-off places, inspiring her dreams and desires. The creature also acts as her subconscious and third eye, helping to plan and visualize what may lie ahead.

Symbolic Healing and Guidance

Element: fire.

Qualities: warm; energetic; charismatic; creative; purposeful; positive; ambitious.

Twos: balance; comfort; self-control; duality; yin yang; stop and go; decisions; choices.

Castle: security; safety; comfort.

Dog: loyalty; energy; adventure; friend; connection.

Sirin: desires; beauty; future planning; intuition; visualization.

Globe: visualization; planning; projection.

Upright Message: The Two of Wands shows a time of methodical planning. Your desires and ambitions have been tended to and you have attained a certain level of stability. You hope to protect your accomplishments while building on them, so this moment provides a nice pause to enjoy dreaming the next stage into being. The world is in your hands and can be shaped accordingly with a little patience and the fire of your will and imagination.

Reversed Message: The Two of Wands always brings choices and decisions in the planning process, and you may be finding difficulty with this aspect. Use this time to go within and reconnect with your vision. Examine your desires and what makes you tick. It is totally fine to slow down and enjoy your comfortable life while you consider your goals. It won't be long before things get moving again, but don't force anything right now. The best outcomes will come after rest.

Three of Wands (Fortune and Favor)

Keywords: expansion; opportunities; action;
fortune; favor; illumination.

Crystal: Fluorite: focus; study; opportunity; expansion; growth; energize.

The woman walks purposefully along the cliffs, leaving her castle far behind. Strong foundations have been built on the liminal space between land and sea, where she can master her place in the wider world. She exudes a sense of confidence and purpose as she strides inland to participate, observe and study more. This card is about putting your plans into action and adding skills to your repertoire. You are working hard to overcome any limitations, and this will be the key to your fortune and success.

The woman holds a wand and is surrounded by two more; the three wands represent consolidation, balance and strong foundations. In the distance, the sea reflects broader horizons and more opportunities to come. In the woman's bag, she carries the tools she might need to develop her skills. Around her neck she wears nature's gifts to show gratitude for the journey she is about to take. The light of the full moon illuminates the way and all along her path wild roses flourish, showing freedom and expansion.

Symbolic Healing and Guidance

Element: fire.

Qualities: warm; energetic; charismatic; creative; purposeful; positive; ambitious.

Threes: balance; solidity; support; divine blessings; consolidation.

Castle: security; starting point; base.

Roses: growth; expansion; exploration.

Upright Message: You are heading into a new phase of self-development. You may be adding to your skill set and seeking out new paths to explore. To do this, you need to push yourself out of your comfort zone and try new things. The time is right to study and explore your interests further. The pathways are open to assure your success in everything you undertake. Be mindful to stay curious, grounded and in gratitude.

Reversed Message: If you find there are constant blocks between you and your goals, do check to see that you have not skipped an important step. Did you put in the work? There may be a skill you overlooked that needs to be added to your repertoire. Have another look at the landscape before you, and seek out those things that enrich your mind, body and soul. The Three of Wands represents a trinity in balance, so all three areas must be taken care of.

Four of Wands (Hame and Hearth)

Keywords: homecoming; stability; family; celebration; accomplishments.
Crystal: Citrine Cluster: joyful connections; belonging; security; grounding and uplifting.

The woman is arriving home after extensive time away during which she has accomplished a great many things. There are stories to tell, but first she wants to drink in all the wonderful sights and sounds of her homeland that sits between the land and the sea. Gulls greet her on the path, calling out in celebration of her arrival. They bear gifts and charms from her family. The charms include a fish for abundance, a ship for opportunity and an anchor for security.

This is an occasion to wear her best coat, embroidered with shells and starfish. As she walks the path, she feels warm and cozy despite the sea breeze coming in off the coast. A proud memorial statue stands on the hill to honor the great many ancestors tied to this place. There is an awareness that she is walking home on a well-worn road, and she stops to pay respects to all the souls who paved the way before her. Later in the evening there will be celebrations, bonfires and feasting by the light of the moon. The four wands will be placed around the perimeter for security and protection.

Symbolic Healing and Guidance

Element: fire.

Qualities: warmth; energetic; charismatic; creative; purposeful; positive; ambitious.

Fours: robust; solid; strong; complete; stable.

Gulls: adaptable; resourceful; family.

Shells: The scallop is often associated with St. James and important pilgrimages.

Starfish: connectedness; reaching out; lucky encounters.

Upright Message: Life feels good. You are ready to celebrate with the people you love the most. Familiar places and comfortable old haunts beckon you. Happy memories filled with joy and laughter rise to the surface and there may be a significant occasion to commemorate. You have achieved a lot and can kick back and relax for a while or connect with others. Catching up is in the cards with no expectations or agendas. Make the time to enjoy your home and heritage.

Reversed Message: You may be quietly working on some aspect of yourself, a personal goal or achievement. You are not ready to share the results yet because it feels very personal, and you might not be at the finish line. Give yourself credit and a pat on the back, maybe even a small treat or reward for now. You are doing so well but you don't want to jump the gun.

When the time is right, make sure you involve others in your celebration. The support and encouragement are there, even if you are unsure of it. Try not to segregate yourself or turn away from family. There may be tensions or unresolved things in the background at home, but your achievements will be welcomed and honored.

Five of Wands (Stane and Sennachie)

Keywords: confusion; opinion; disagreement; verbal sparring; conflict.
Crystal: Blue Lace Agate: calmness and communication.

The sennachie is an ancient storyteller in the oral tradition. She moves from village to village telling tales of honor and valor, or perhaps scaring the children with stories of supernatural beings that hide in the woods. Here, she wears a painted mask of woad to dramatize her expressions. There is a certain expectation from the sennachie to entertain and elaborate or hugely exaggerate the rumors of unrest in the royal courts. The people know that there is a fine line between news and theater.

In this card, the sennachie asks that you take a closer look at your own drama. Once we start believing the tales we spin then it becomes all too easy to defend them vigorously. Opinions can so easily turn to conflict and misunderstanding. Five wands rise up sharply protecting the sennachie from such attacks. Within the realm of the storyteller such "truths" are there for documentation, debate and speculation. Differing perspectives can be interesting to explore if they are not harmfully rigid and without humor.

The stone marks the gathering space where the sennachie asks us to step into her world and suspend belief for a while. We are required to play by her rules in this space and conduct ourselves in noble opposition if debate arises. The wise owl looks over proceedings hoping to instill wisdom. In Greek mythology, owls were thought to protect those heading into battle, so here he brings calm to proceedings. The hare represents the shape-shifting nature of truth as it darts around, changing with perception. This card is a reminder to stop, listen and exchange without conflict.

Symbolic Healing and Guidance

Element: fire.

Qualities: warm; energetic; charismatic; creative; purposeful; positive; ambitious.

Fives: conflict; discord; miscommunication; rivalry.

Owl: wisdom; protection.

Hare: shifting; changing.

Stone Monolith: meeting place; common ground; community; exchange; safe space.

Upright Message: There has been a lively clash of ideas with frustrations mounting and tempers rising. Ask yourself what stories are being told and what underlying beliefs are being rigorously defended. How can you shift your own perspective to calm things? Getting into a conflict when beliefs are so ingrained is futile. The Five of Wands asks that you remain calm, engage in conscious listening and avoid unnecessary conflict.

Reversed Message: You may be unclear of your views right now and feel unable to take part in debate or have a valid voice. This can leave you vulnerable to attack or provocation; or you may find yourself passionately defending an ideology that is unstable or lacking in substance. It is perfectly okay to concede and declare a lack of knowledge. It is also okay to not be persuaded until you have the full story. Beware of being led astray by lazy speculation or idle gossip.

Six of Wands (Silt and Silver)

Keywords: success; confidence; accolades; recognition.
Crystal: Pyrite: success; self-worth; confidence.

A woman sits by the mouth of the harbor in contemplation. Around her are six wands showing that she has accumulated success and material worth but is also generous and responsible.

Her biggest accomplishment is that she is self-assured in her dealings and knows her own mind. This has taken lots of hard work, self-examination and also analyzing the views of others. You could say she has arrived at her authentic self and is being recognized for her contributions and achievements. The curve of the harbor wall surrounds her, protecting her. The little fishing cottages represent community support and admiration. This is a time when people have her back and they can be relied on. There is recognition from peers and the wider community and a further showing of respect. The woman is dressed in elegant clothing and wears the finest fabrics from far-off lands. Her belts and buckles are adorned with purses and exotic amulets. They represent the exchange of ideas and her intelligent trades in the world. A feline companion shows her independence and self-confidence. Two row boats in the harbor signify her exchanges with the wider world and how she can continue to make progress with her own hard work and self-motivation.

Symbolic Healing and Guidance

Element: fire.

Qualities: warm; energetic; charismatic; creative; purposeful; positive; ambitious.

Sixes: abundance; balance; stability.

Cat: independence; self-confidence.

Fish (Silver Darlings): wealth; success.

Village: community; recognition.

Upright Message: You have reached a point of great achievement and success in some endeavor. You have overcome barriers and perhaps confusion and conflict to stand self-assured in accomplishments of your own making. You can be proud of how far you have come, and to your surprise and delight, others are recognizing your contributions and celebrating with you. You may be open to receiving additional rewards and recognition at the moment. The wider world is seeing what you have to offer and beckons you to come and participate.

Reversed Message: Perhaps you feel overlooked at the moment. Success and acclaim are being diverted elsewhere and maybe others are taking the recognition for your achievements. Although disheartening, it is time to dust yourself off and re-examine your ideas around success and achievement. Do you seek approval from others? Are you feeling unworthy of being seen or are you hiding behind impostor syndrome? Perhaps you try too hard to win or are unnecessarily competitive. Once you can shine a light on the things that hold you back then others will come to your support, and you will step into the arena of respect and admiration.

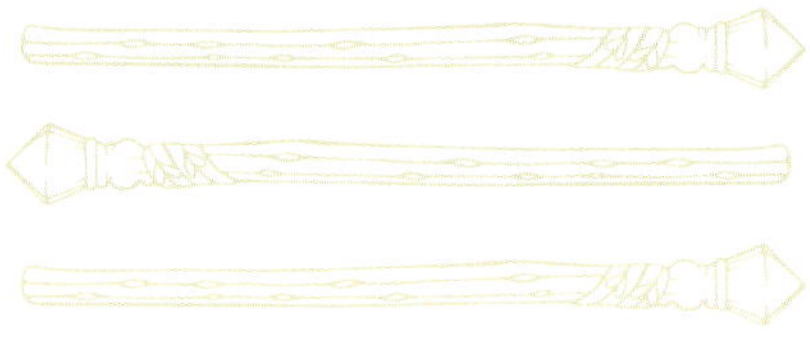

Seven of Wands (The Frontier)

Keywords: challenges; protection; defense; determination.
Crystal: Spirit Quartz: protection for person and land; harnessing fear.

The woman stands strong in this scene, wielding a double-ended wand in front of her as a defense to anyone wishing her harm. A homestead has been built on her land and she has reached a point of comfort and security in her life. There was a certain amount of complacency and now it seems she has attracted unwanted attention or unkind thoughts from others who covet what she has. Initially surprised at this unprovoked confrontation, she has taken matters into her own hands.

Becoming aware of the situation, she is well prepared to ward off the attacks. The other six wands form a protective barrier around her and in front of her home. The wands all carry depictions of animals and mythical beasts who lend their unique medicine to the tasks at hand. The bear, the snake, the boar, the goat, the fox and the dragon all make an appearance to assist her. In her skirts nestles a scaly armadillo that represents physical and spiritual protection.

Symbolic Healing and Guidance

Element: fire.

Qualities: warm; energetic; charismatic; creative; purposeful; positive; ambitious.

Sevens: obstacles; challenges.

Bear: compassionate protection; great mother energy.

Snake: good vs. evil; transformative energy.

Boar: confronting fears; overcoming adversity.

Goat: determination; vitality; sure-footed; confidence; all-around vision.

Fox: intuitive; psychic; wise; cunning; trickster; teacher.

Dragon: courage; fortitude; righteous; supported by magic.

Upright Message: The Seven of Wands indicates that you have put your head above the parapet and have attracted the attention of a person or people who want what you have. They may be motivated by envy, insecurity or a false sense of entitlement. Either way, it is a surprise and a jolt to your comfortable existence because now you have to protect yourself and your success. Try to use all the skills you have at your disposal to understand how this person operates. Their own lack of awareness rather than malicious intent might become dangerous if not rigorously refuted. You will overcome.

Reversed Message: You may sense a constant bombardment of negative energy from outside sources. This could be constant criticism, confrontation, displays of jealousy, sarcasm or random attacks. This hostility can be exhausting, and you may be feeling upset and confused about why you are being targeted this way. You have let your defenses down, so you need to gather your courage and strength to address these attacks. Come out of victim mode and proactively clear this negativity to protect yourself spiritually and physically if needed.

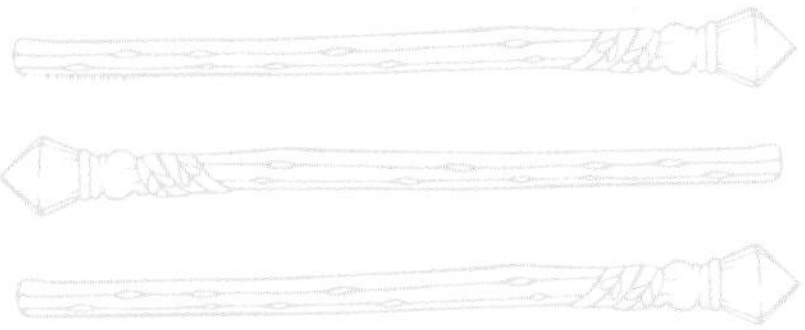

Eight of Wands (Ariel)

Keywords: movement; quickening; divine support.
Crystal: Angelite: dispelling fear and anxiety; removing emotional blockages; growing self-awareness.

An angelic being moves swiftly through the night sky lit by glittering stars. Eight beautiful wands fly through the darkness, speeding forward in growing momentum. The Eight of Wands card shows that you have learned strength and resolve. You can now move forward with ease on your journey; it is time to soar. Below, a river winds its way through the landscape, nourishing the land. A grand castle sits in waiting to show all that can potentially be attained. Spiritual help is on your side and divine wings carry you closer to your goals and dreams.

The angel carries bells and amulets that assist quickening and attract good fortune. On her hand, pointing to the future, she bears the infinity sign, indicating that you will experience infinite success on the road you are on.

Symbolic Healing and Guidance

Element: fire.

Qualities: warm; energetic; charismatic; creative; purposeful; positive; ambitious.

Eights: strength; prosperity; infinite success.

Bell: clarity; synchronicity; frequency; higher vibration.

Bird: messenger; good news; joy.

Flower: beauty; creativity; growth.

Fish: good fortune; flow.

Shell: direction; being on the right track.

Geode: uncovering hidden treasures; discovery.

Leaf: new beginnings; winds of change.

Upright Message: You are entering a highly productive phase. Be focused and ready for everything that comes your way. You will find this busy period very exciting and rewarding. It feels like you are blessed with good fortune and magical synchronicity. There will be no obstacles in your way and people are eager to meet you and learn from you. It feels like a quickening and accumulation of so many things coming to fruition.

Reversed Message: It could be that things are going too fast for you to handle. Your focus is scattered, and this is when stress sets in. Start to prioritize, make lists and take one thing at a time. There is every indication that success will be forthcoming if you take a deep breath and gather your thoughts.

Nine of Wands (The Ascendant)

Keywords: persistence; stamina; struggle; survival.
Crystal: Moss Agate: boosts immunity; strength; persistence; endurance; healing; recovery.

The woman standing at the foot of a steep hill has come a great distance and has faced many challenges. As the uphill climb looms, she is becoming battle weary and wounded, but still determined and holding strong. Her wounds have been tended to and her face is painted and battle ready. The nine wands rise up in her path to show it won't be easy and there will be new barriers to face. But her cloaks and cap carry the emblem of two phoenix birds and bull horns to show how determined she is. One of the phoenix birds rises up defiantly and the other leans down toward its mate, holding an olive branch. They represent surrender and rebirth, a lesson we learn as we stop struggling against our own will and just do what is necessary.

Nine of Wands is about survival and rising to the challenge in the face of adversity. It shows us a way to take each moment as it comes, with gratitude, focus and intention. The struggles of the nine are close to completion and close to profound spiritual rewards.

On one of the wands sits a butterfly to show how transformative this process is with the end almost in sight. At the top of the hill there is a cairn illuminating the darkness. A certain level of enlightenment is coming even if it can't be reached quite yet.

Symbolic Healing and Guidance

Element: fire.

Qualities: warm; energetic; charismatic; creative; purposeful; positive; ambitious.

Nines: inner strength; big lessons; enlightenment.

Phoenix: rising; survival; immortality; rebirth; knowledge; transformation; fire.

Butterfly: transformative energies.

Upright Message: Just when you think the challenges are too much to bear, the Nine of Wands asks you to trust, surrender and carry on. Somehow you will feel a surge of inner strength and the motivation to make that last effort. In this greatest of tests, you are being prepared for the ultimate rewards. Although you are exhausted and only able to concentrate on getting through the next step, the way is being paved for peace and true awakening.

Reversed Message: The barriers may feel too strong and the challenges too numerous. They seem to come from so many directions right now that you may doubt that you have it in you. Certainly, there might be a crisis of confidence that threatens to make you give up. Have faith and be reminded that this is your final big test. You will make it through, and you will soon reach your destiny.

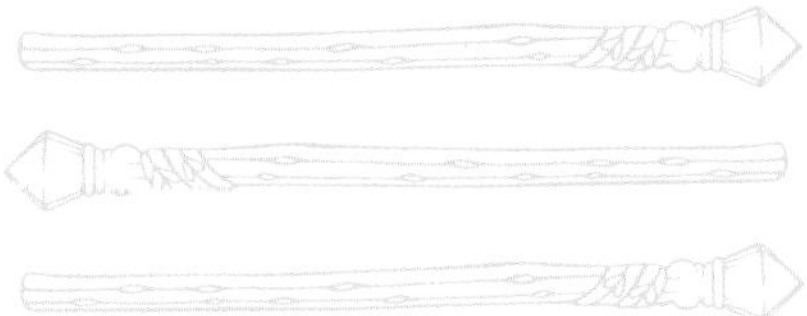

Ten of Wands (The Journey)

Keywords: completion; journey; achievement; effort; assessment.
Crystal: Smoky Quartz: grounding; protecting; energizing; absorbs negative energies.

A man is carrying a collection of ten wands on his back. Each one represents a trial and tribulation as well as a lesson learned. They are heavy to carry but he is so close to his destination now and can see a welcoming village just over the rise.

There are no more great hills to climb now, but the final walk requires some additional effort. He feels positive and supported knowing there is not far to go.

There are signs of nearing the finish line. Embroidered into his clothing are symbols depicting good health, wisdom, love, balance, transformation and enlightenment. Various amulets and charms hang on his backpack to support this journey he has been on. They represent the higher manifestations of the skills he has accumulated on the way. They include a spiral, corn doll, key, hourglass, pendulum, bell, compass, cross, scroll and coin purse.

The Ten of Wands signifies a great journey coming to an end and a sense of relief and quiet anticipation for the future. With this card comes a period of meditation and contemplation.

Symbolic Healing and Guidance

Element: fire.

Qualities: warm; energetic; charismatic; creative; purposeful; positive; ambitious.

Tens: completion; accomplishment; content.

Caduceus: healing.

Cat and Dog: love; loyalty; family.

Eye: enlightenment.

Dragonfly: transformation.

Corn Doll: abundance.

Key: opportunity.

Hourglass: change; progress.

Pendulum: mystery; prophecy.

Bell: clarity; higher vibration; positivity.

Compass: direction; hope; inspiration.

Cross: faith; spirituality.

Scroll: knowledge; study; communication.

Coin Purse: wealth; prosperity.

Upright Message: You have been working extra hard to reach your goals. Maybe you have added additional responsibility or study. You know that rewards and a more peaceful time lie ahead. This card can signal an accumulation of skills and experiences that are very beneficial to you. Soon, you will be able to reap the rewards, but just make sure you do not feel overburdened. It may be time to let go, delegate and hand over some responsibilities.

Reversed Message: Perhaps you feel overburdened and a bit overwhelmed by your success and productivity. Work can often just create more work. You might see a gentler pace of life ahead if you could break the cycle. It's a great time to evaluate how you have been doing things. Can you figure out how to work smart and share the load?

Page of Wands (The Messenger)

Keywords: dreams; inspirations; transformative meditation.
Crystal: Mookaite: inner and outer balance; inspirations; creativity; aspirations.

The page is dreaming things into reality. Part of their initiation and study will include meditation and exploration of the dream worlds where they receive most of their inspiration.

A key is held loosely, showing many experiences to be unlocked and much potential yet to be fulfilled. The single wand shows inspiration and divine creativity unfolding. Little moths flutter up from the rich foliage representing thoughts becoming actions. A robin flies past in the foreground, a messenger of hope and good things to come. This page is dressed in rich fabrics with woven layers and florals showing fertile imagination and unfolding potential.

The Page of Wands signals new beginnings, creative thinking and developing passions.

Symbolic Healing and Guidance

Element: fire.

Qualities: warm; energetic; charismatic; creative; purposeful; positive; ambitious.

Pages: apprentice; potential; creative energy.

Robin: hope; good fortune; dreams; passions.

Moths: divine inspiration; thoughts and ideas.

Wool/Weave: fates; discovery; uncovering.

Upright Message: The Page of Wands represents a calling to follow your dreams and passions. There may be deeper spiritual momentum driving your thoughts and ideas. Right now, you are free to imagine and explore the possibilities, even though you don't know how you will get there. It is a great time to study further or seek out a mentor.

Reversed Message: You may be feeling scattered or unsure of your purpose. There are too many thoughts and ideas running around your head and they all hold desire and appeal. Since you are on the cusp of starting something new, it is fine to experiment and do some soul searching. You might still need to find out what your passions and purposes are. Take your time to explore new hobbies and interests. This is a time of discovery and seeking.

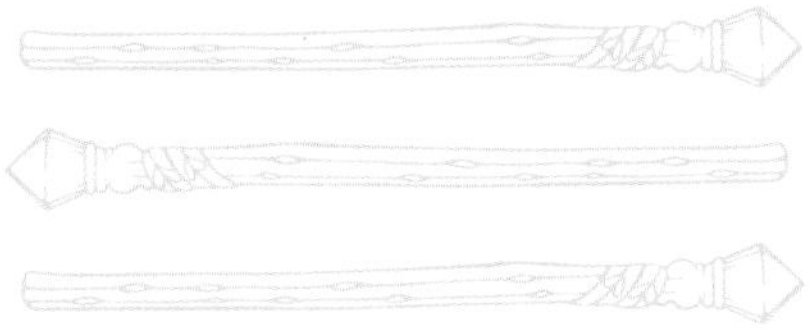

Knight of Wands (Elen of the Ways)

Keywords: action; impulsive; courage; protector.
Crystal: Peridot: balance and harmony.

The Knight of Wands is represented by Elen of the Ways, ancient protector of the roads and the ley lines running through our land. Her steed is a mighty stag who is full of energy and vitality. Impulsive and earthy, he is able to charge right into the heart of things if needed, but he is also strategic and skittish if retreat is required. This knight is a traveler bearing good news and messages from spirit. Weaving their way through the land, they pull energy from the earth and work in service wherever they are needed. They wear the expansive colors of purple for mystery and spirituality, and yellow for optimism and enlightenment. Elen holds a staff bearing an amethyst wand, which connects her to the earth but also enhances intuition and psychic ability. Around her neck, she wears an amulet of moonstone, which acts as a cosmic guide and peridot for balance. Two birds flit by in the foreground, leading the way.

Symbolic Healing and Guidance

Element: fire.

Qualities: warm; energetic; charismatic; creative; purposeful; positive; ambitious.

Knights: action; vitality; service; honor.

Stag: vitality; strategy; royalty; ancient wisdom.

Moths: divine inspiration; thoughts and ideas.

Birds: messengers; leaders.

Upright Message: The Knight of Wands represents a quest and a calling. Ideas become actions and there is spontaneity, movement and travel. This knight is a protector, a guide and a guardian who comes to assist when new ideas are in their fledgling stage. They will help you with messages from spirit and divine inspiration. You may be particularly intuitive right now, feeling in touch with nature and the energies of the land.

Reversed Message: In this position, there is a potent energy waiting to be harnessed. You may be frustrated and wanting to charge ahead but caution is called for and you will get better results when exercising patience and strategy. The Knight of Wands indicates that you can be of great service to nature and humanity, but first you must explore the deeper mysteries of both. Elen asks you to come on a journey to the deepest parts of your soul's calling to discover the potential of your being. A pause in proceedings will bring even more understanding to your quest.

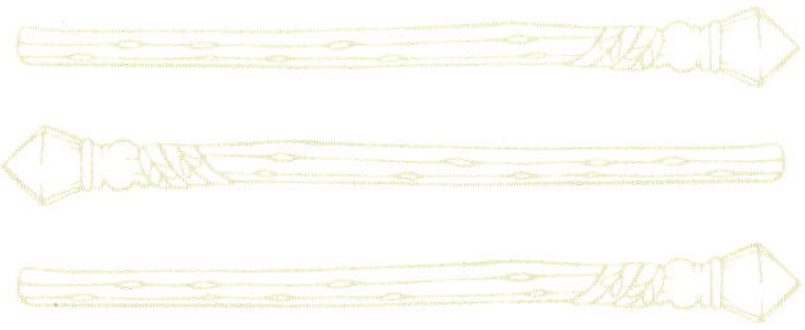

Queen of Wands (Queen of Confidence)

Keywords: confident; sociable; independent.
Crystal: Bloodstone: strength; courage; nobility.

Seated comfortably on her throne, the Queen of Wands is confident, poised and alert. On her throne, there are carved lions representing courage and strength. In one hand she holds her wand, which sprouts a fern, showing new life. In the other hand she cradles a vibrant bouquet of three sunflowers, showing her sunny disposition and social aptitude. The sunflower motif is also echoed on her purse, showing abundance and infinite wealth. The number three also indicates spiritual support, stability and balance. Around the scene, bees hover and are mirrored in her crown; they represent the sun, fertility, creativity and life source.

This queen has a black cat companion who is comfortable sitting in her lap. This shows she has mastered and become comfortable with the dual aspects of herself. The scene personifies both night and day, and there is an abundance of feline energy to represent her bold and carefree nature as well as her hidden depths and inquisitive side. The Queen of Wands is both sociable and curious; she balances her inner and outer worlds well. The high hills give her a sense of seclusion and protection. The ship moored nearby is ready to take her out into the world at a moment's whim. This queen does everything on her own terms while charming and entertaining her subjects in the right measure.

Symbolic Healing and Guidance

Element: fire.

Qualities: warm; energetic; charismatic; creative; purposeful; positive; ambitious.

Queens: feminine; mature; nurturing; ruler.

Sunflowers: sunny disposition; sociable.

Bees: creativity; fertility.

Black Cat: mystery; duality; regal; comforts.

Lions: power; confidence; fierce; independence.

Upright Message: The Queen of Wands brings courage and confidence into your realm. She assists with projects and situations where you need to be bold and innovative. The gifts of communication, diplomacy and social magnetism are given freely. The situation brings new experiences and personal growth where you can lead and also collaborate in a gracious manner. You are self-assured in your beliefs and are able and willing to mentor.

Reversed Message: You may be feeling a bit withdrawn and lacking in confidence. The appearance of this queen provides reassurance and support for you to find your truths and your authentic voice. In particular, she encourages you to get back out there and build your contacts and social engagements.

King of Wands (King of Knowledge)

Keywords: leadership; success; innovator; entrepreneur; progressive.
Crystal: Tiger's Eye: courage; strength; protection; dynamic energy.

The King of Wands sits in an elaborate throne, which displays the ouroboros, showing his infinite power unfolding in the world. He holds out a single wand and roses blossom over his throne symbolizing the cyclical nature of life. This king has the knowledge of the universe at his fingertips and is able to harness it in the real world. To symbolize secret knowledge and esoterica, there is a hidden key and corresponding keyhole in his throne. This king is self-assured and charismatic in his demeanor. He is flanked on either side by two lions, showing his integrity and loyalty to his subjects. This king also has strong values and a keen interest in family and fairness. In the foreground sits a lizard showing curiosity, agility and intellectual dexterity. There is a passion for people and their involvement in his business. He enjoys seeking out knowledge and counsel and will find new and innovative ways to lead responsibly.

Symbolic Healing and Guidance

Element: fire.

Qualities: warm; energetic; charismatic; creative; purposeful; positive; ambitious.

Kings: masculine; mature; generous; ruler.

Ouroboros: infinite; universal laws; potential.

Lions: regal; integrity; creativity; fertility; power.

Lizard: curious; good luck; dexterity.

Roses: abundance; fertility; cycles.

Key: mystery; knowledge.

Upright Message: You will find that this king brings in the opportunity to lead and take control in the creative realm. It is all about having the right team and expertise to help you visualize and manifest your goals fully. The King of Wands sees the worth in others and enjoys engaging them in the process. In many ways he is a great humanitarian leader who likes to rule fairly but with passion and fire.

Reversed Message: In the reversed position, you may be asked to temper the aspects of this king that are spiraling out of control. Passion, fire and visionary zeal can sometimes spill into aggression and control. The charisma and charm represented in this card can lean toward lazy delegation and manipulation if left to its darker agenda. Observe how you can balance out these traits and transmute them into more inspired and visionary leadership. See how you can get more comfortable with yourself and less stressed. Be like the King of Wands who meets his challenges with flair and good humor.

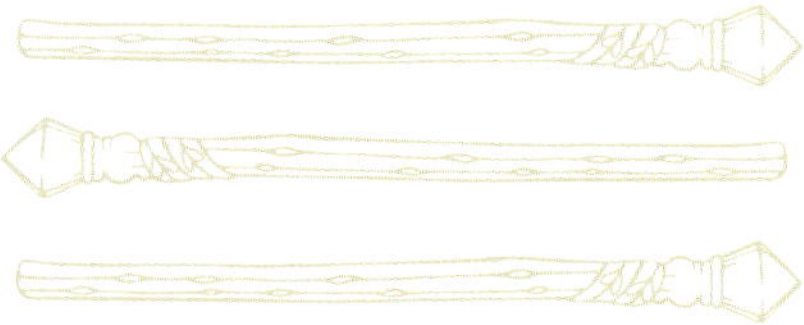

Using the Cards

This tarot deck lends itself very well to most spreads as well as stand-alone meditations, daily inspirations and affirmations. Outlined here are three of Anita's favorite layouts.

Universal Folk Tarot will happily interact with other tarot and oracle decks in your spreads, especially Universal Folk Oracle. Nature and crystal-based decks are highly recommended for compatibility.

Single Card Meditation

A single card selected will point to a theme, or give a gentle reminder for the inquirer to use as a focus for the day or week. This consultation can be carried on your person or displayed in a favorite place or altar setting.

Crystals are a particular favorite meditation tool and can be used to amplify the cards and assist with their mood or meaning.

Three-Card Spread

Most commonly representing past, present and future influences in divination, the three-card spread can give a quick overall consultation.

The Celtic Cross Spread

This traditional layout can give a more in-depth consultation and divination.

S - Signifier/Querent

1 - Situation

2 - Barriers and Obstacles

3 - Present Influences-Conscious

4 - Underlying Energies-Subconscious

5 - Immediate Past

6 - Immediate Future

7 - Your Energy/Attitude

8 - Others Energy/Environment

9 - Hopes and Fears

10 - Potential Outcomes

About the Author/Artist

Anita Inverarity is a full-time visual artist from North East Scotland. She lives with her life partner Phil and two feline friends in a rural farmhouse, which is also a home studio and gallery, near the Banffshire coast.

Describing her work as "Universal Folk" in its presentation and aesthetic, she weaves pattern and rich symbolism to create an imaginative new world inspired in part by folk art, myth and heritage. Using the traditional drawing mediums of ink pens and watercolor pencil to conjure mysterious characters and animal companions, Anita is most at home in front of her drawing board. Her other interests include exploring the natural world, history, music, and of course, tarot.

Acknowledgements

A List of People, Places and Mythology

Forever Intertwined with Universal Folk Tarot

Thank you to Jamie McCloy and Kima cat for inspiring the Magician.

Thank you to Koshka and AM Broome for inspiring Two of Wands.

Thank you to M Arner for inspiring the Empress.

Thank you to my jeweler friend, Victoria Markham, at Silver Orb (UK) for creating so many beautiful pieces inspired by my work. You can find some of the jewelry represented in the following cards:

the Magician; the High Priestess; the Lovers; Ace of Wands; Knight of Wands; Two of Cups; Five of Cups; Six of Cups; Queen of Cups; Six of Pentacles.

Mythology references include: The Fin Folk of Orkney in the Hierophant; Norse mythology in the Chariot and Page of Pentacles; Roman mythology in the Wheel of Fortune; Egyptian mythology in Justice and the Two of Cups; Faerie lore from Scotland and Ireland in the Devil; Myths from Scottish, Celtic and the ancient British Isles in the Nine of Pentacles, Three of Swords, Knight of Wands and Five of Wands; The Hawaiian goddess Pele in Judgment; Sedna from Inuit mythology in the Five of Pentacles; Sirin from Russian Mythology.

Landscapes setting the scene include: Aquhorthies Stone Circle and Bennachie mountain range (NE Scotland) in The Hermit; Dunnottar Castle (NE Scotland) in the Three of Wands; Stonehaven Harbour (NE Scotland) in the Seven of Wands; Craigievar Castle (NE Scotland) in the Eight of Wands; The Uffington White Horse (Oxfordshire, England) in the Eight of Cups.